THE BACCHAE OF EURIPIDES

A COMMUNION RITE

THE BACCHAE
OF EURIPIDES

A COMMUNION RITE

by Wole Soyinka

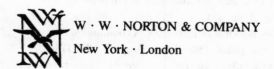

W · W · NORTON & COMPANY
New York · London

Library of Congress Cataloging in Publication Data
Soyinka, Wole.
    The Bacchae of Euripides: a communion rite.
    I. Euripides. Bacchae. English. II. Title.
[PR9387.9.S6B3   1974]   882'01   74-9501
ISBN 0-393-04396-7

2 3 4 5 6 7 8 9 0

Introduction

Some lines in this version of *The Bacchae* will be familiar to those who are acquainted with the Yoruba deity; Ogun, god of metals, creativity, the road, wine and war. They come both from traditional praise-chants and from my long poem *Idanre*, the latter written in celebration of Ogun's night of pilgrimage. The following passage from an earlier essay of mine, *The Fourth Stage**, explains why this was predictable.

'The Phrygian god and his twinhood with Ogun exercise irresistible fascination. His thyrsus is physically and functionally parallelled by the *opa Ogun* borne by the male devotees of Ogun. But the thyrsus of Dionysos is brighter, it is all light and running wine, Ogun's stave is more symbolic of the labours of Ogun through the night of transition. A long willowy pole, it is topped by a frond-bound lump of ore which strains the pole in wilful curves and keeps it vibrant. The bearers, who can only be men, are compelled to move about among the revellers as the effort to keep the ore-head from weighting over keeps them perpetually on the move. Through town and village, up the mountain to the grove of Ogun, this dance of the straining phallus-heads pocks the air above men and women revellers who are decked in palm fronds and bear palm branches in their hands. A dog is slaughtered in sacrifice, and the mock-struggle of the head priest and his acolytes for the carcass, during which it is literally torn limb from limb, inevitably brings to mind the dismemberment of Zagreus, son of Zeus. Most significant of all is the brotherhood of the palm and the ivy. The mystery of the wine of palm, bled straight from the tree and potent without further ministration, is a miracle of nature acquiring symbolic significance in the Mysteries of Ogun. For it was instrumental to the tragic error of the god and his sequent passion. . . . Ogun, in proud acceptance of the need to create a challenge for the constant exercise of will

* from *The Morality of Art* ed. D. W. Jefferson.

and control, enjoins the liberal joy of wine. The palm fronds are a symbol of his wilful, ecstatic being'.

The Bacchae belongs to that sparse body of plays which evoke awareness of a particular moment in a people's history, yet imbue that moment with a hovering, eternal presence.

Pieced together, the following historical canvas emerges: A new industrial economy had begun to replace the agrarian on Mainland Greece and in her colonies and in the outlying areas of Asia Minor. Silver and gold mines were opened up and with them, a group consciousness among urban labour which evolved naturally from the broken phrateries. A series of wars had displaced peasants in their thousands and forced them to seek a living in the mines and in the rising war industry. Such labour migrations, as in the contemporary instance of the Americas and the Indies, brought with them their customs and religions; the immigrants maintained their observances in varying degrees of syncretism and purity. Slaves and displaced peasants, confronted by the often unbearable reality of a new environment, adapted the old beliefs and customs without surrendering basic tenets or diluting their spiritual intensity. The Dionysian evangelism commenced not surprisingly in Thrace and Phrygia which, until the rivalry of Attica, remained the principal mines of Asia Minor. And when, in the wake of the wars of Greek colonialism, the mining industry expanded in Attica, a similar Dionysiac movement swept through mainland Greece, becoming deeply entrenched as the Persian invasion increased the ruinous displacement of the peasants.

The dionysiac impulse was not new. Dionysianism, essentially agrarian in origin, was the peasant's natural evocation of, and self-immersion in, the mysterious and forceful in Nature. The Dionysiac is present, of course, in varied degrees of spiritual intensity in all religions. But primarily Dionysiac cults found suddenly fertile soil in Greece after centuries of near-complete domination by state-controlled Mysteries because of peasant movements in the wake of urban expansion. The definitive attachment to a suitable deity – in this case Dionysos – was nothing more than the natural, historic process by which populist movements (religious or political) identify themselves with mythical heroes at critical moments of social upheaval. Myth is part wish-fulfilment through hero projections. This means, naturally, that it is an outline for action, especially for groups within society who have experienced loss and deprivation. The cleverer tyrants such as Periandros and Kleisthenes recognised this potential and, for their own hardly altruistic motives, actively encouraged the spread of Dionysiac 'rage'.

Dionysos (or Zagreus, Sabazius and a dozen other eponymous variations) was eminently suited to the social and spiritual needs of the new urban classes. His history was extravagantly rich in all the ingredients of a ravaged social psyche: displacement, suppression of identity, dissociation, dispossession, trials and the goal of restoration. As deity also of the moist elements he fulfilled the visceral link of the peasant personality to Nature rhythms, his experience of growth, decay and rejuvenation – in short, the magic and mystery of life. As a non-Olympian he was easy, even natural to identify with. His followers could become truly *entheos*; his worship released the pent-up frustrated energy of all the downtrodden. In challenging the state Mysteries he became champion of the masses against monopolistic repressions of the 'Olympian' priesthood, mercantile princes and other nobility. The myths which grew up around him, the new elaborations on his traditional origins should therefore be read as statements of intent. Certainly, the threatened classes did not fail to see them as such.

Guthrie observes: 'It is a small but significant point that in all later stories of the persecution of Dionysos, the offending mortal is punished by the god whom he has wronged and who appears in power and might to wreak his own vengeance.'* A possible conclusion which appears to escape Guthrie, however, is the significance of that social reality from which such later emendations

* W. K. C. Guthrie, *The Greeks and their Gods.*

arose. The slaves, helots and urban working classes are not yet strong enough to cast themselves in the role of protagonists of vengeance for the suppressed deity. Punishment descends from the god himself or, in a special application of the principle of poetic justice, is administered by a member of the impious nobility. Often it is self-inflicted. *The Bacchae* conforms to this usage; with this escape Euripides could hardly be charged with popular incitement even though the message is clearly subversive. For *The Bacchae* is not a play of accommodation but of group challenge and conflict. The political accommodation that came later (Apollo cedes the shrine to Dionysos for a few months every two years), this attested compromise makes *The Bacchae* an aetiological drama within the social struggle.

There is an unfortunate element of distortion in Thompson's claim that 'in the ritual of the Orphic brotherhoods . . . by eating the flesh and drinking the blood of the bull Dionysos, men whom the class-struggle had humbled and oppressed fed on the illusion of a lost equality'.* Such a claim contradicts the positive character of the native solidarity that was experienced by the Dionysiac communicants. Where religion became an instrument of exploitation for the alliance of priesthood and nobility it also, with long delayed justice, proved the foundering rock for their monopolistic strength. And this came about only when a new or resurrected religion appeared, that neither fed nor fed on the illusions of the oppressed.† Such a religion thrived best when it represented godhead as inseparable from Nature. All religions of vegetation deities conform to this requirement. Their cults and observances are dedicated to regenerating earth and stimulating growth. Land, the primary economy and primary stimulant of communal labour, its mystery of seasonal fluctuation, dearth and bounty is the natural base of vegetation religions. Material (harvest) benefits

---

* George Thompson, *Aeschylus and Athens.*

† A parallel error is the familiar one of the once traditional explanation of that ritual of plantation slaves, where performers dressed up and 'aped' the hierarchic pretensions of their masters.

which derived from land were identified with spiritual rewards. Where the ritual responsibility for land renewal lay with a small elite, the economic powers of such a minority were limitless. A religion which transferred its ritualism to communal participation and identified self-renewal with the truth of land renewal and food production fed, not on illusion, but on a long repressed reality. As a social force, its powers were incalculable.

The impact of the Dionysiac revival on the slave-sustained economy of Greek society becomes understandable within this context. Punishment for 'economic sabotage' – malingering, rebelliousness, quota failure etc. etc. – was, in a sense, a disciplinary perversion of the nature-propitiation principle. At least it must have appeared so to the classes who, in the rural phase, provided the scapegoat in time of plague or famine. This selected sacrifice was ritualistically fed, whipped on the genitals with wild branches and led in procession through the city. He was then burnt to death and his ashes were scattered to the winds. This effort to stimulate growth must have struck the oppressed groups as hardly different from the 'public deterrent' – public flogging, breaking on the wheel etc. etc. – meted out to the mine-worker who had ruined a piece of machinery, attempted to foment labour unrest or reduced the week's profit in some other way. Both forms of imposed penance were designed to stimulate greater productivity. What the class-conscious myths of Dionysos achieved was to shift the privilege for the supply of scapegoats to the classes which had already monopolised all other privileges. The magic munificence of Nature requires both challenge and sacrifice in all nature renewal myths; Pentheus, the aristocrat, provides both in the highly seditious version by Euripides.

The fusion of socio-religious strands in a myth re-told 'in terms of fifth-century conflicts'* makes the puzzle largely artificial which finds it strange that Euripides, an acknowledged iconoclast, cynic, rationalist and democrat should turn in his very last years to write a play that appears to run contrary to his rationalist

* Dodds, Introduction to *The Bacchae*.

insights, a drama of passionate magic that, it is often claimed, smacks of a deathbed conversion. It must be conceded howevever that the visceral quality of *The Bacchae*, its dramatic energy and religious ferocity, provokes amazement on such lines. No other play of his, and few others among extant Greek drama are so thoroughly impregnated with image and essence of human passage in conflict and resolution: life itself and death; womb and destroyer; order and chaos (inchoate essence); ecstasy and serenity; hubris and humility; the visceral and formalistic . . . the list is endless. Its totality: a celebration of life, bloody and tumultuous, an extravagant rite of the human and social psyche. Certainly there is a hint, if not of religious fanaticism, at least of a manic religious inspiration suddenly let loose.

It is therefore this very quality which creates instances of dissatisfaction in this play. The ending especially, the petering off of ecstasy into a suggestion of a prelude to another play. But *The Bacchae* is not an episode in a historical series, and this is not merely because Euripides did not live to write the next instalment. The drama is far too powerful a play of forces in the human condition, far too rounded a rite of the communal psyche to permit of such a notion. I have therefore sought a new resolution in the symbolic extension of ritual powers, but only such as we have already encountered with the Bacchantes on the mountain-side. The disruptive challenges to Nature that have been let loose in the action demand no less. Agave's final understanding is an exteriorised god-submission only on the level of itemised *dramatis personae*; it is far more fundamentally a recognition and acceptance of those cosmic forces for which the chorus (the communal totality) is custodian and vessel in the potency of ritual enactment. Admission of her last, aberrant mind after the enormous psychic strain of a wilful challenge (also a necessity for evoking the maximum powers), this last in-gathering releases the reluctant beneficence of Nature.

I see *The Bacchae*, finally, as a prodigious, barbaric banquet, an insightful manifestation of the universal need of man to match himself against Nature. The more than hinted-at cannibalism corresponds to the periodic needs of humans to swill, gorge and copulate on a scale as huge as Nature's on her monstrous cycle of regeneration. The ritual, sublimated or expressive, is both social therapy and reaffirmation of group solidarity, a hankering back to the origins and formation of guilds and phratries. Man re-affirms his indebtedness to earth, dedicates himself to the demands of continuity and invokes the energies of productivity. Re-absorbed within the communal psyche he provokes the resources of Nature; he is in turn replenished for the cyclic drain in his fragile individual potency.

ACKNOWLEDGMENTS

A twenty-year rust on my acquaintanceship with classical Greek
made it necessary for me to rely heavily on previous translations
for this adaptation of *The Bacchae*. Two versions which deserve
especial mention, in that I have not hesitated to borrow phrases
and even lines from them, are those by Gilbert Murray,
published by Allen and Unwin, London, and Oxford University
Press, New York; and William Arrowsmith, published in
Euripides Five: Three Tragedies, edited by David Grene and
Richard Lattimore, by University of Chicago Press. My
publishers and I gratefully acknowledge the publishers
concerned for the use I have made of these translations.

EURIPIDES

B.C.

480 or   Born, probably on the island of Salamis, where his family
485   had a property. Euripides was Athenian and was the son of
         Mnesarchus (or Mnesarchides) and Cleito, whose home
         was at Phlya, east of Hymettus.

454   First production of *Peliades**.

453   Gains his first victory at the Dionysiac Festival with
         Peliades. Unlike Sophocles, Euripides only gained five
         victories (four in his lifetime and one posthumously).

?   *Rhesus**. If this extant play is to be attributed to Euripides
         it is an early work, but there is a school of thought that it is
         more probably a fourth-century work.

438   *Alcestis, Cressae*, Telephus*, Alcmaeon in Psophis**.

431   *Medea, Philoctetes*, Dictys*, Theristae**.

430   *Children of Heracles.*

428   *Hippolytus.*

427   *Andromache.*

424   *Hecuba.*

422   *Suppliants.*

418   *Heracles Furens.*

415   *Trojan Women, Alexander*, Palamedes*, Sisyphus**.

413   *Electra.*

412   *Helen, Andromeda**.

411   *Iphigeneia in Tauris.*

410   *Ion.*

411–09 *Phoenician Women, Oenomaus*, Chrysippus**.

408   *Orestes.*
         Leaves Athens to live in the Court of Archelaus, King of
         Macedonia.

407–6   Dies in the winter, exiled in Macedonia.

405   *Bacchae, Iphigeneia in Aulis, Alcmaeon in Corinth** (pos-
         thumous production).

There is no evidence of a date for the production of the satyr-play,
Cyclops.

* *indicates lost plays.*
The italicised dates are established.

CAST LIST

SLAVE LEADER

OLD SLAVE

SLAVE CHORUS

HERDSMAN

DIONYSOS

MASTER OF REVELS

VESTALS

PRIESTS

FLOGGERS

TIRESIAS

KADMOS

FIRST BACCHANTE

WEEPING BACCHANTE

OTHER BACCHANTES

PENTHEUS

OFFICER

AGAVE

BRIDE

BRIDEGROOM

BRIDE'S FATHER

FATHER-IN-LAW

BESTMAN

SERVANT-GIRL

WEDDING GUESTS

CHRIST-FIGURE

THREE WOMEN

PRODUCTION NOTE

The Slaves and the Bacchantes should be as mixed a cast as is possible, testifying to their varied origins. Solely because of the 'hollering' style suggested for the slave Leader's solo in the play, it is recommended that this character be fully negroid.

This version of *The Bacchae* has been conceived as a communal feast, a tumultous celebration of life. It must be staged as such. Any cuts in the text, dictated by production necessities must NOT be permitted to affect the essential dimension of a Nature feast.

The Bacchae of Euripides was first presented by the National Theatre company at the Old Vic on August 2nd 1973 with the following cast:

DIONYSOS	Martin Shaw
PENTHEUS, KING OF THEBES	John Shrapnel
TIRESIAS	Julian Curry
AGAVE, PENTHEUS' MOTHER	Constance Cummings
CADMUS, AGAVE'S FATHER	Paul Curran
HERDSMAN	David Bradley
GUARD	Desmond McNamara
OFFICER	Gawn Grainger
LEADER OF THE BACCHANTES	Isabelle Lucas
LEADERS OF THE SLAVES	Ram John Holder
	Leslie Rainey
OLD SLAVE	Harry Lomax

BACCHANTES
Sarah Atkinson, Rachel Davies, Carol Drinkwater, Chrissy Iddon, Jennifer Piercey

SLAVES, BODYGUARDS, ETC
David Firth, John Gregg, Paul Gregory, Mary Griffiths, James Hayes, Richard Howard, Desmond McNamara, Clive Merrison, Maggie Riley, James Smith, Michael Stroud, Stephen Williams

PERCUSSION
Laurie Morgan

PRODUCTION	Roland Joffé
DESIGN	Nadine Baylis
LIGHTING	Leonard Tucker
MUSIC AND SOUND	Marc Wilkinson
MOVEMENT	Malcolm Goddard

THE BACCHAE OF EURIPIDES
A COMMUNION RITE

To one side, a road dips steeply into lower background, lined by the bodies of crucified slaves mostly in the skeletal stage. The procession that comes later along this road appears to rise almost from the bowels of earth. The tomb of Semele, smoking slightly is to one side, behind the shoulder of this rise. Green vines cling to its charred ruins.

In the foreground, the main gate to the palace of Pentheus. Farther down and into the wings, a lean-to built against the wall, a threshing-floor. A cloud of chaff, and through it, dim figures of slaves flailing and treading. A smell and sweat of harvest. Ripeness. A spotlight reveals DIONYSOS *just behind the rise, within the tomb of Semele. He is a being of calm rugged strength, of a rugged beauty, not of effeminate prettiness. Relaxed, as becomes divine self-assurance but equally tensed as if for action, an arrow drawn in readiness for flight.*

DIONYSOS. Thebes taints me with bastardy. I am turned into an alien, some foreign outgrowth of her habitual tyranny. My followers daily pay forfeit for their faith. Thebes blasphemes against me, makes a scapegoat of a god.

It is time to state my patrimony – even here in Thebes.

I am the gentle, jealous joy. Vengeful and kind. An essence that will not exclude, nor be excluded. If you are Man or Woman, I am Dionysos. Accept.

A seed of Zeus was sown in Semele my mother earth, here on this spot. It has burgeoned through the cragged rocks of far Afghanistan, burst the banks of fertile Tmolus, sprung oases through the red-eyed sands of Arabia; flowered in hill and gorge of dark Ethiopia. It pounds in the blood and breasts of my wild-haired women, long companions on this journey home through Phrygia and the isles of Crete. It beats on the walls of Thebes, bringing vengeance on all who deny my holy origin and call my mother – slut.

He looks down on the clouds of smoke wrapped round his feet, rising from the tomb. He scuffs the ground with a foot, scattering ashes and sparks.

Something lives yet, there is smoke among the rubble. Live embers. The phoenix rises and that is life – wings from cooling cinders, tendrils from putrefaction, motion from what was petrified . . . There are green vines on the slag of ruin. Mine. As on the mountain slopes, clustering and swelling. They flush, they flood the long-parched throats of men and release their joy. This sacrament of earth is life. Dionysos.

From the direction of the 'crucifixion slope' comes a new sound, a liturgical drone – lead and refrain, a dull, thin monotone, still at some distance. A HERDSMAN *carrying a jar darts across the stage to the threshers.*

DIONYSOS *stands still, statuesque.*

HERDSMAN. I think I hear them coming.
SLAVE LEADER (*eagerly seizes the jug and takes a swig*). What did you say?
HERDSMAN. The Masters of Eleusis. They've begun the revels.

The SLAVES *gather round and listen. The jug is passed round.*

SLAVE LEADER (*spits*). Revels!
HERDSMAN. Which of us is the victim this year?

SLAVE. That old man of the king's household. The one who looks after the dogs.

HERDSMAN (*shrugs*). He's old enough to die.

SLAVE LEADER. He had better survive!

HERSDMAN (*fearfully*). Sh-sh!

SLAVE LEADER. I have said it before. If another of us dies under the lash ...! (*The jug is passed to him again. He takes a long draught, sighs.*) There is heaven in this juice. It flows through my lips and I say, now I roll the sun upon my tongue and it neither burns nor scorches. And a scent-laden breeze fills the cavern of my mouth, pressing for release. I know that scent. I mean, I knew it once. I live to know it once again.

HERDSMAN. I think I understand you. Forget it, friend.

SLAVE LEADER. A scent of freedom is not easily forgotten. Have you ever slept, dreamt and woken up with the air still perfumed with the fragrance of grapes?

HERDSMAN. There is no other smell at this time of the year. If you live in the hills, that is. It gets oppressive sometimes, to tell the truth. You know, rather cloying.

SLAVE LEADER. Surrounded by walls one can only dream. But one day ... one day ...

HERDSMAN. Not you. No one will ever trust you outside of the city walls. Dissimulation is an art you will never master. You need the sly humility, the downcast eye. Yes Sire, King Pentheus, no sir, Honourable Eunuch of the Queen's Bed-chamber ...

SLAVE LEADER. Let's speak of better things. Tell me of those hidden vineyards. They are like my buried longings. I know each precious acre of the forbidden terrain, inch by inch. And I know I envy you. The air of Thebes is sterile. Nothing breathes in it. Nothing – really – lives. Come closer ... distend your nostrils ... now breathe in, deeply ... smell!

HERDSMAN. Look, if every time I bring you wine you have to ...

SLAVE LEADER. Do you smell anything? Anything at all? After the hills and the vines and the wind can you smell me? Do I live?

HERDSMAN. You promised . . .

SLAVE LEADER (*makes an effort, takes a deep breath*). What does it matter anyway. An open-air slave or a walled-up slave . . . we all fold our arms and thank the gods for a generous harvest.

HERDSMAN. Generous is not the word for it. The vines went mad, so to speak; they were not themselves. Something seemed to have got under the soil and was feeding them nectar. The weight that hung on the vines even from the scrubbiest patch, each cluster . . . (*his hands shape them*) pendulous breasts of the wives of Kronos, bursting all over with giant nipples.

SLAVE LEADER. I felt it on my tongue. The sun has left the heavens and made a home within the grapes of Boetia.

HERDSMAN. You may say that. It was a joy to tread them.

The liturgical drone is now very close.

They are nearly here. I must go.

SLAVE LEADER. Wait. (*Takes hold of him.*) Suppose the old man dies?

HERDSMAN. We all have to die sometime.

SLAVE LEADER. Flogged to death? In the name of some unspeakable rites?

HERDSMAN. Someone must cleanse the new year of the rot of the old or the world will die. Have you ever known famine? Real famine?

SLAVE LEADER. Why us? Why always us?

HERDSMAN. Why not?

SLAVE LEADER. Because the rites bring us nothing! Let those to whom the profits go bear the burden of the old year dying.

HERDSMAN. Careful. (*He points to the row of crosses.*) The palace does not need the yearly Feast of Eleusis to deal with rebellious slaves. (*He takes the jug and turns to go.*)

SLAVE LEADER. Look, tell them on the hills, tell your fellows up there . . .

HERDSMAN (*instantly rigid*). What?

SLAVE LEADER (*hesitates, sighs*). Nothing. Tell them – we also are
waiting.

The HERDSMAN *goes off the same way as he entered. Led by a
solemn figure who is the* MASTER OF REVELS, *a procession emerges
and proceeds over the rise.*

First, the MASTER OF REVELS, *next black-robed* PRIESTS *intoning
a liturgy, punctuated by hand-bells. After them come a group of*
VESTALS *in white. The first pair carry fresh branches; the middle
section garlands and flowers; the last pair carry bowls. The* VESTALS
are followed by an old man, TIRESIAS, *completely white-bearded,
dressed in what might approximate to sackcloth-and-ashes, who
carries a bunch of used twigs. Behind him are four stalwart figures in
red, armed with strong, supple lashes. At every three or four paces
the* PRIESTS *ring their bell, upon which the two maidens in front of*
TIRESIAS *turn and sprinkle him with what might be ashes or chaff,
while the four men lay into him from all sides with their whips. A
straggle of crowd follows. This sedate procession passes through and
around* DIONYSOS *without seeing him and proceeds downstage
towards the gates of the palace. The* SLAVES *have stopped work and
are watching.*

A small ceremony of 'cleansing' is performed on the palace gate. The
PRIESTS *take branches from a bundle borne by the two leading girls,
symbolically scouring the gates with them, then pile the used twigs on
the bunch already borne by* TIRESIAS. *He is sprinkled and flogged as
before.*

At the sight of TIRESIAS, *there is distinct surprise and agitation
among the* SLAVES.

Suddenly TIRESIAS *appears to wilt, collapse. A further stroke of the
lash brings him to his knees. The intoning continues without stopping,
and the lashes.*

As he falls prone, a bright flash reveals DIONYSOS *on the tomb of
Semele. All action ceases. The music of* DIONYSOS.

DIONYSOS (*smiling*). Sing Death of the Old Year, and – welcome the new – god.

A prolonged, confused silence. In the threshing-hut the SLAVES *forcefully restrain their* LEADER *who seems bent on giving immediate vocal acknowledgement to the god.*

SLAVE. You'll get us killed. We'll be wiped out to a man.
ANOTHER. Remember the helots. Don't be rash.

DIONYSOS *comes down among the procession. The* PRIESTS *retreat in terror as he turns towards the* VESTALS.

DIONYSOS. And the vestals of Eleusis?
VESTALS (*hesitant and fearful*). We . . . welcome the new . . . god.
DIONYSOS. Oh, but joyfully, joyfully! Welcome the new god. Joyfully. Sing death of the old year passing.
VESTALS (*liturgical, lifeless*). Welcome the new god. Joyfully. Sing death. . . .

They stop, look at one another foolishly. One or two begin to titter and DIONYSOS *bellows with laughter. The* VESTALS *regain some relaxation.*

DIONYSOS. And now try again. Together, with joy.
VESTALS (*courageously*). We . . .

A VESTAL *detaches herself from the group, her eyes riveted on the face of* DIONYSOS. *She scoops up a garland as she passes the flower-bearers and comes up to the stranger. He bows his head and she garlands him.*

VESTAL. Welcome the new . . .

Keels over in a faint and is caught by DIONYSOS. *Carrying her he moves towards the* PRIESTS.

DIONYSOS. And now the priests of Eleusis?
PRIEST. We welcome . . .
ANOTHER. . . . a miracle, a miracle.

They hurriedly edge their way out and flee in the direction from which they made their entry. The FLOGGERS *also retreat a little way, watchful.*

SLAVE LEADER (*breaking loose after the* PRIESTS' *retreat*). Welcome the new god! Thrice welcome the new order! (*Hands cupped to his mouth, he yodels.*) Evohe-e-e-e! Evoh-e-e-e!

The sound is taken up by echoes from the hills. It roves round and round and envelops the scene. All heads turn outwards in different directions, listening. A mixture of excitement and unease as the sound continues, transformed beyond the plain echo to an eerie response from vast distances.

From the same responsive source, intermingled strains of the music of DIONYSOS. *It swells inwards to the attentive listeners. The* VESTAL *in the arms of* DIONYSOS *stirs, responding. She lowers herself to the ground slowly, moves into a dance to the music. As the dance takes her close to the* SLAVE LEADER *he moves away with her; the dance soon embraces all the* VESTALS *and* SLAVES.

DIONYSOS, *smiling, slips off as they become engrossed in the dance. The music stops, the enchantment is cut off. The fainting* VESTAL *looks round her in growing panic.*

VESTAL. Don't leave us!

She runs out in pursuit, the other VESTALS *following.*

SLAVE LEADER. Let's follow.

The SLAVES *hang back. The euphoria has melted rapidly.*

SLAVE. I think we've gone too far already.
SLAVE LEADER.
    You hesitant fools! Don't you understand?
    Don't you *know*? We are no longer alone –
    Slaves, helots, the near and distant dispossessed!
    This master race, this much vaunted dragon spawn
    Have met their match. Nature has joined forces with us.

Let them reckon now, not with mere men, not with
The scapegoat bogey of a slave uprising
But with a new remorseless order, forces
Unpredictable as molten fire in mountain wombs.
To doubt, to hesitate is to prove undeserving.

SLAVE. There is such a fault as rashness.

SLAVE LEADER.
When the present is intolerable, the unknown
Harbours no risks.

ANOTHER SLAVE. I don't know ... why make ourselves con-
spicuous. Let the free citizens of Thebes declare for this
stranger or against him.

SLAVE LEADER. Whose interest will direct their choice? Ours?

SLAVE. No, but ...

The SLAVES *look away from one another, uncomfortable but afraid.
After an awkward silence, the* SLAVE LEADER *sighs in defeat.*

SLAVE LEADER. Let us go as far as the gates then. We should
know at least how the Thebans receive him. In our own interest.

They follow him out, guiltily.

TIRESIAS *is left alone with the floggers. As he begins to pick himself
up painfully, they rush forward to help him up. He brushes them off
angrily.*

TIRESIAS. Take your hands off!

He rises, tries to dust himself and winces.

FIRST FLOGGER. Were you hurt?

TIRESIAS. Animals!

FIRST FLOGGER. Oh, We ... didn't mean to.

TIRESIAS. You never do.

SECOND FLOGGER. Who was he?

FIRST FLOGGER. Yes who was he? Where did he spring from?

TIRESIAS (*snorts*). Who was he? Where did he spring from?

Fools! Blind, stupid, bloody brutes! Can you see how you've covered me in weals? Can't you bastards ever tell the difference between ritual and reality.

FIRST FLOGGER. I was particularly careful. I pulled my blows.

TIRESIAS. Symbolic flogging, that is what I keep trying to drum into your thick heads.

FOURTH FLOGGER. I could have sworn I only tapped you gently from time to time.

THIRD FLOGGER. It's all that incantation. It soaks in your brain and you can't feel yourself anymore.

TIRESIAS. I suppose you would have carried on like you do year after year. Flogged the last breath out of my body.

THIRD FLOGGER (*among shocked protests*). How could you think such a thing? You are not a slave. I mean, we do have some control.

TIRESIAS. Yah, you showed it. Anyway what are you standing there for?

FIRST FLOGGER. Well ... we ... I mean, we don't quite know what to do.

THIRD FLOGGER. I mean, it's a bit of a departure, isn't it? Never known anything like this happen before. Well damn it, who was he?

FOURTH FLOGGER. And the vestals, gone with him.

TIRESIAS. Go after them. You've been cheated of your blood this time so your throats are a little parched. Go up in the mountains and you'll find other juices to quench your thirst.

FIRST FLOGGER (*irritated*). You will speak in riddles!

TIRESIAS. The feast has shifted to the mountains – is that simple enough?

FIRST FLOGGER (*wearily*). Just tell us what we are now expected to do when we get there?

TIRESIAS. Whatever you wish. Just take your violent presences away from me!

THIRD FLOGGER. Well, that's plain enough.

FIRST FLOGGER. You know who he was.

TIRESIAS (*draws himself up*). Since when has it been the custom for common no-brain wrestlers to cross-examine the seer of Thebes.

FIRST FLOGGER. Let's go. (*They exit.*)

TIRESIAS. Swine! (*He feels his body tenderly, then shouts.*) Wait! Which of you kept my staff?

DIONYSOS (*re-enters*). Borrow my thyrsus.

TIRESIAS. Thank you. Dionysos I presume?

DIONYSOS. You see too well Tiresias.

TIRESIAS. As if the gentlest emanations from the divine maestro would not penetrate the thickest cataract.

DIONYSOS. Yet there is one here who has no defect in his eyes but will not see.

TIRESIAS. I know him. Handle him gently Dionysos, if only for his grandfather's sake.

DIONYSOS. Kadmos was pious. Consecrating this ground in memory of my mother at least kept her alive in the heart of Thebes ... but that is Kadmos. Let every man's actions save or damn himself. We shall see what Pentheus chooses to do.

TIRESIAS (*shrugs*). I knew that would be the answer. Anyway, thank you for stepping in just now. You were just in time.

DIONYSOS. Were you really in trouble?

TIRESIAS. I was. One can never tell how far the brutes will go. Mind you, I took the precaution of wearing your fawn-skin under my gown. You see how the sackcloth has been flogged to ribbons. I had to collapse to remind them they were getting carried away again.

DIONYSOS. But what made the high priest of Thebes elect to play flagellant?

TIRESIAS. The city must be cleansed. Filth, pollution, cruelties, secret abominations – a whole year's accumulation.

DIONYSOS. Why you? Are you short of lunatics, criminals or slaves?

TIRESIAS. A mere favour to Kadmos whom I love like a brother.

Kadmos is Thebes. He has yielded all power to Pentheus but I know he still rejoices or weeps with Thebes. And Thebes – well, let's just say the situation is touch and go. If one more slave had been killed at the cleansing rites, or sacrificed to that insatiable altar of nation-building . . .

DIONYSOS. Quite a politician eh Tiresias?

TIRESIAS. A priest is not much use without a following, and that's soon washed away in what social currents he fails to sense or foresee. As priest and sage and prophet and I know not how else I am regarded in Thebes, I must see for the blind young man who is king and even sometimes – act for him.

DIONYSOS. And if you have been torn to pieces at the end, like an effigy?

TIRESIAS. Then I shall pass into the universal energy of renewal . . . like some heroes or gods I could name.

DIONYSOS. Go on.

TIRESIAS. Isn't that it? Is that not why Dionysos?

DIONYSOS. Is that not what?

TIRESIAS. Why you all seem to get torn to pieces at some point or the other?

DIONYSOS. Don't change the subject. Go on about you.

TIRESIAS. I've said it all. What more do you want me to say?

DIONYSOS (*he moves close to* TIRESIAS, *tugs gently at his beard*). Poor Tiresias, poor neither-nor, eternally tantalised psychic intermediary, poor agent of the gods through whom everything passes but nothing touches, what happened to you in the midst of the crowd, dressed and powdered by the hands of ecstatic women, flagellated by sap-swollen birches? What sensations coursed your withered veins as the whips drew blood, as the skin of the birches broke against yours and its fragrant sap mingled with your blood. You poor starved votary at the altar of soul, what deep hunger unassuaged by a thousand lifelong surrogates drove you to this extreme self-sacrifice. Don't lie to a god Tiresias.

TIRESIAS. I never lie. I told you the truth.

DIONYSOS. Yes, but only a half-truth, like your prophecies. Tell me the rest.

TIRESIAS (*Cornered. Finally*) Yes, there was hunger. Thirst. In this job one lives half a life, neither priest nor man. Neither man nor woman. I have longed to know what flesh is made of. What suffering is. Feel the taste of blood instead of merely foreseeing it. Taste the ecstasy of rejuvenation after long organising its ritual. When the slaves began to rumble I saw myself again playing that futile role, pouring my warnings on deaf ears. An uprising would come, bloodshed, and I could watch untouched, merely vindicated as before, as prophet. I approach death and dissolution, without having felt life . . . its force . . .

DIONYSOS. Not even just now?

TIRESIAS. You forget. That goes by rote. Ecstasy is too elusive a quarry for such tricks. Even if I did sacrifice a few drops of blood.

DIONYSOS (*lays his hands gently on* TIRESIAS' *shoulders*). Thebes will have its full sacrifice. And Tiresias will know ecstasy.

TIRESIAS. Something did begin. Perhaps those lashes did begin something. I feel . . . a small crack in the dead crust of the soul. Listen! Can you hear women's voices? Strange, just then I almost felt my veins race.

DIONYSOS (*drawing back*). Dance for me Tiresias. Dance for Dionysos.

TIRESIAS. That's like asking the elephant to fly. I've never danced in all my life.

The music of DIONYSOS *is heard.* TIRESIAS *stands entranced for some moments, then moves naturally into the rhythm, continues to dance, rapt.*

DIONYSOS *watches for a while, then slips off.*

Enter KADMOS *who stands amazed and watches.* TIRESIAS *senses his presence after a while and stops, clutching his thyrsus defensively.*

TIRESIAS. It's someone else. Who is it?

KADMOS. Your good friend, Kadmos of the royal house. How goes it with you Tiresias? Are you well?

TIRESIAS. You must be blind to need to ask such a question.

KADMOS. Well I confess I do not believe my eyes.

TIRESIAS. Oh Kadmos Kadmos, how I wish you were still King of Thebes.

KADMOS. That's not like you to wish undone what is already done. What's biting you?

TIRESIAS. Your grandson, the foolish, blind, headstrong, suicide-bent king.

KADMOS. Not suicide-bent I hope. His faults I readily admit. But what's he done now?

TIRESIAS. Nothing yet. It's what he's going to do. I know how it will all end. Oh Kadmos, wisdom is what we need in a king at this moment, a sense of balance and proportion.

KADMOS. You didn't seem a model of proportion when I came on you a moment ago. What did you think you were doing?

TIRESIAS. Saving Thebes again, though I fear that is too late. It is far far easier to save Thebes from the anger of disgruntled classes than from the vengeance of a spited god. Neither your piety nor my new-found ecstasy can help him now.

KADMOS. Tiresias, you know I have no head for conundrums . . .

TIRESIAS. Yes, your son takes after you there. But at least you don't go at every riddle with sledgehammer and pitchfork.

KADMOS. Is there yet another danger that threatens Thebes?

TIRESIAS. None that you or I could help. (*Sounds in the distance.*) Listen to them! Can you hear that? Can you feel the power of it, Kadmos?

KADMOS (*the significance dawns on him*). But – you are not with them. You promised me Tiresias! You promised Thebes.

TIRESIAS. What you hear is another sound, a new order. Your *other* grandson took my place. The wanderer has come home. He's here. (*The* BACCHANTES *enter to shouts of* 'Bromius

Evohe-e! Zagreus!) Quickly. Stand aside and be silent. They sound already possessed. (*They hide themselves.*)

BACCHANTE. Where?

ANOTHER. Where?

ANOTHER. Where?

ANOTHER. Where?

That cry is taken up, repeated fast from mouth to mouth, ending with a long, impassioned communal cry.

BACCHANTES. Br-o-o-o-o-mius!

BACCHANTE. Bromius . . .

ANOTHER. Bromius . . .

ANOTHER. Bromius . . .

Again the name is tossed from tongue to tongue, beginning as a deep audible breath and accompanied by spasmodic, scenting movements. It swells in volume and breaks suddenly into another passionate scream by the leader of the BACCHANTES.

FIRST BACCHANTE.

Bro-o-o-o-o-mius! Be Manifest!

Be manifest Bromius, your Bacchantes have taken the field.

You've led us. Lead us now.

ANOTHER.

We've journeyed together. Through Lydia and Phrygia . . .

ANOTHER.

Over rivers of gold, Bactrian fastness . . .

ANOTHER.

Through slopes of the clustering vine.

ANOTHER.

Companion of forest and towered cities

Of the steppes of Persia and wastes of Media

ANOTHER.

Through the dance of the sun on Ethiopia's rivers

Lakes, seas, emerald oases.

ANOTHER.
    Rooting deep, ripeness and mysteries
    Rooting as vine in the most barren of soils
FIRST BACCHANTE.
    The silvering firs have trembled, we have seen rockhills
    Shudder, earth awaken, ramparts of heaven cave
    Beasts answer from their lairs, sap rise in the trees
    And the sevenfold bars on the gates of Thebes
    Splinter – at the Maenads' cry of BROMIUS!
BACCHANTES.
    Evohe-e-e-e-e-e!

Re-enter the SLAVES.

SLAVE LEADER (*in a ringing voice*). Bacchantes, fellow strangers, to this land.

A gradual hush. They turn towards the sound.

SLAVE LEADER. Fellow aliens, let me ask you – do you know Bromius?

The women turn to one another, still in a haze of possession, but astonished at such a ridiculous question. One or two continue to moan, completely oblivious to the interruption.

FIRST BACCHANTE. Do we *know* Bromius?
SLAVE LEADER. Bromius. Zagreus. Offspring of Zeus as the legend goes.
FIRST BACCHANTE (*over a general peal of laughter*). Stranger, do *you* know Bromius.
SLAVE LEADER. A god goes by many names. I have long been a spokesman for the god.
FIRST BACCHANTE. And yet you ask, do we know Bromius. Who led us down from the mountains of Asia, down holy Tmolus, through the rugged bandit-infested hills of the Afgans, the drugged Arabian sands, whose call have we followed through

the great delta? Who opened our eyes to the freedom of desert sands? To the liberation of waters? Do we know Bromius?

SLAVE LEADER. Do you love his worship?

FIRST BACCHANTE.

Hard are the labours of a god

Hard, but his service is sweet fulfilment.

SLAVE LEADER (*coming forward*). Then make way. (*They part and he comes among them.*)

WEEPING BACCHANTE (*the fainting Vestal*). What is it? What does the slave want with us? I want my god, the son of Zeus.

ANOTHER. Where shall we seek him? Where find him?

SLAVE LEADER. Fall back a little. Seal up the streets and let no one intrude. There is a hymn all believers know.

Pause. The BACCHANTE *sizes him up, decides for him.*

FIRST BACCHANTE. Let every mouth be silent. Let no ill-omened words profane your tongues.

SLAVE LEADER.

It is the hour we have long awaited.

What is hidden must some day come to light

Now, raise with me the old old hymn to godhead.

The CHORUS *intone beneath the prayer.*

FIRST BACCHANTE.

Blessed are they who know the mysteries of god

Blessed all who hallow their life in worship of god

Whom the spirit of god possesses, who are one

With earth, leaves and vine in the holy body of god.

Blessed are the dancers whose hearts are purified.

Who tread the hill in the holy dance of god.

Blessed are they who keep the rites of the Earth-Mother

Who bear the thyrsus, who wield the holy wand of god

Blessed are all who wear the ivy crown of god

Blessed, blessed are they: Dionysos is their god.

CHORUS.
> Blessed, blessed, thrice blessed are we:
> Dionysos is our god.

The first chords of music, oriental strings and timbrels.

WEEPING BACCHANTE. Bromius, Bromius . . .
SLAVE LEADER.
> Blessed are they who bathe in the seminal river
> Who merge in harmony with earth's eternal seeding
> Blessed they whose hands are cupped to heaven
> Their arms shall be funnel for the rain of understanding
> Blessed are all whose feet have trodden the dance of grapes
> Whose hands have nursed the vine, earth's gentlest binding
> Blessed their joys in the common sacrament, whose beings
> Open to intuitions in the liberation of the grape
> Blessed, thrice blessed the innocence of acceptance
> The arms that reach to a welcome of god
> Blessed, thrice blessed, the moment of recognition
> Of god without as the essence within.

CHORUS.
> Blessed, blessed, thrice blessed are we:
> Dionysos is our god.

SLAVE LEADER.
> For he is the living essence of whom, said Heaven
> The seed is mine, this seminal germ
> Earthed in sublimation of the god in flesh
> The flesh in god. I bind my seed in hoops of iron
> And though all seek him, safe I hold him
> Safe in the loins wherefrom he sprang.
> Let all revere the gracious earth,
> Womb of the infant deity.

WEEPING BACCHANTE. Bromius, Bromius . . .
SLAVE LEADER.
> Tribute to the holy hills of Ethiopia
> Caves of unborn, and the dark ancestral spirits.

Home of primal drums round which the dead and living
Dance. I praise the throbbing beat of the hide
The squeal and the wail of flutes . . .

BACCHANTES (*moaning*). Oh Bromius, Bromius.

FIRST BACCHANTE.

It is fallen to me at last, fallen
All fallen to me from the raving satyrs
Fallen at last to me to celebrate his name;
Dionysos! Stranger, honey-voiced
Spokesman of my god. Tell us tales of what you know,
Sing to me again of Dionysos.

Music. It has the strange quality – the nearest familiar example is the theme-song of 'Zorba the Greek' – with its strange mixture of nostalgia, violence and death. The scene which follows needs the following quality: extracting the emotional colour and temperature of a European pop scene without degenerating into that tawdry commercial manipulation of teenage mindlessness. The lines are chanted not sung, to the musical accompaniment. The SLAVE LEADER *is not a gyrating pop drip. His control emanates from the self-contained force of his person, a progressively deepening spiritual presence. His style is based on the lilt and energy of the black hot gospellers who themselves are often first to· become physically possessed.*

The effect on his crowd is, however, the same – physically – as would be seen in a teenage pop audience. From orgasmic moans the surrogate climax is achieved. A scream finds its electric response in others and a rush begins for the person of the preacher. Handfuls of his clothes are torn, his person is endangered but he never 'loses his cool'. As his chant approaches climax a sudden human wave engulfs him and he is completely submerged under screaming, 'possessed' lungs and bodies. As with such scenes there is always something of an overall ugliness about the manifested emotion. But the radiant isolated votive or two or even the few faces of intensely energised spiritual rapture that stands out in the melée indicate something of the awesome depths of this self-release.

SLAVE LEADER.

Then listen Thebes, nurse of Semele,
Crown your hair with ivy
Turn your fingers green with bryony
Redden your walls with berries.
Decked with boughs of oak and fir
Come dance the dance of god.
Fringe your skins of dappled fawn
With wool from the shuttle and loom
For the looms are abandoned by throngs of women
They run to the mountains and Bromius before
They follow the violent wand of the bringer of life
The violent wand,
Of the gentle, jealous, joy!

BACCHANTES (*like a wail*). Bromius, Bromius . . .

SLAVE LEADER (*progressively radiant*).

He . . . is . . .
Sweet upon the mountains, such sweetness
As after-birth, such sweetness as death.
His hands trap wildness, and breed it gentle
He infuses tameness with savagery.
I have seen him on the mountains, in vibrant fawn-skin
I have seen his smile in the red flash of blood
I have seen the raw heart of a mountain-lion
Still pulsing in his throat
In the mountains of Eritrea, in the deserts of Libya,
In Phrygia whose copper hills ring with cries of
Bromius, Zagreus, Dionysos.
I know he is awaited, the covenant, promise,
Restorer of fullness to Nature's lean hours.
As milk he flows in the earth, as wine
In the hills. He runs in the nectar of bees and,

In the duct of their sting lurks – Bromius.
Oh let his flames burn gently in you, gently,
Or else – consume you it must – consume you . . .

CHORUS. Bromius . . . Bromius . . .

SLAVE LEADER.

His hair a bush of foxfires in the wind
A streak of lightning his thyrsus
He runs, he dances,
Kindling the tepid
Spurring the stragglers
And the women are like banks to his river –
A stream of gold from beyond the desert –
They cradle the path of his will.

CHORUS. Come, come Dionysos . . .

SLAVE LEADER.

Oh Thebes, Thebes, flatten your wall.
Raise your puny sights
To where the heights of Kithairon await you

CHORUS. Yes, yes . . .

SLAVE LEADER.

On the slopes where Dionysos will come
Run free with you in your labour of song
Your dancing drudgery, your chores of dreaming –
In the truth of night descends the secret –
Hold, enbrace it.

CHORUS. Yes yes . . . set me free . . . set me free.

SLAVE LEADER.

The sun touches the vines on the slopes
And *that* is godhead. Dew falls on the grass
And *that* is godhead. The sap awakens –
A birth,
A dawn,
A spring
Pure dewdrops down the mountain
That is godhead. And you

Nestled in earth's womb are
Green leaves in winter, woodsap in snow
You are the eternal ivy on the wand of life
Emerald pines that defy the winter
Dates of the oases in the drought of deserts.

BACCHANTES. Bromius . . . Bromius . . .

SLAVE LEADER.

Seek him in your breasts with love, within
Your hidden veins, in the quiet murmur of your blood
Seek him in the marrow, in wombstone, he is fount
Of life. He made an anvil of the mountain-peaks
Hammered forth a thunderous will, he farmed the slopes
And the vine tempers his will. In plains and valleys
Nest his joyful Bacchae, his mesh of elements
Reconciles a warring universe.

BACCHANTES. Come Bromius, come . . .

SLAVE LEADER.

He is the new life, the new breath, creative flint
Flood earth with his blood, let your shabby streets
Flow with his life, his light, drum him into the heart
Like thunder. He is the storehouse of life
His bull horns empower him
A bud on the autumn bough, he blossoms in you
His green essence fills your womb of earth . . .

BACCHANTES. Bromius . . . Bromius . . .

SLAVE LEADER.

There is power in your thyrsus, feel!
It pulses. Feel! It quivers and races with sap.
Throat, tongue, breast, calling forth the powers of life
Hold him, embrace him. His dance covers you
His drums envelop you, your skin is one with his drum
Tuning and straining tight. Spindle and shuttle
In your hand – behold – the wand of god
The hearthstone his thyrsus, thrusting from earth
The fire is tamed in new greenery of life

In fawn-skin and ivy, and the thorn of life
Piercing your blood. . . .!

A long scream from a BACCHANTE *snaps the last restraint on the women. They rush the* SLAVELEADER *and engulf him. He disappears underneath. From under the melée of limbs, the wild, desperate chant of 'Where? Where? Where?' recommences, diminishing as the mass of flesh is unravelling, dispersed in different directions, groping, unseeing. Other* SLAVES *drag the* SLAVE LEADER *to safety. The chant continues faintly, off, for some time after they have all disappeared.*

Cautiously KADMOS *and* TIRESIAS *emerge.* KADMOS *is in a high state of excitement.*

KADMOS. Why are we waiting. Let's go, let's go.

TIRESIAS. Where?

KADMOS. To the mountains, where else? Let's go and do him honour.

TIRESIAS. But are you dressed?

KADMOS *flings off his cloak, revealing the dionysian fawn skin under it.*

KADMOS. Aren't I? (*Takes* TIRESIAS' *hand.*) Here, feel that. You won't find finer foreskin except on Dionysos himself.

TIRESIAS. He isn't circumcised?

KADMOS. Who? Who isn't circumcised?

TIRESIAS. Dionysos. What you said about his foreskin.

KADMOS. Did I? Slip of the tongue.

TIRESIAS (*considers it quite seriously*). I wonder how many of that you'd need to make a Bacchic smock.

KADMOS. If that was what Dionysos demanded . . . a couple of thousand slaves forcibly circumcised . . . Pentheus could arrange it.

TIRESIAS. Not for Dionysos.

KADMOS. I suppose not. Anyway how come you to think of such things in the first place?

TIRESIAS. You said it, not me.

KADMOS. All right, all right. I said it was a slip of tongue. Quite natural at my age.

TIRESIAS. It's not natural at your age, that's the point. I found that significant. It's not natural at all.

KADMOS. When you start on significances you lose me.

TIRESIAS. You are a wily one. Fancy hiding your Bacchic togs under a cloak. You shook me when you first came in, all that pretence as if you were shocked at the sight of me dancing.

KADMOS. Oh that, I was merely testing my own resolve. Kadmos, Kadmos, it doesn't befit your age and rank – so I kept telling myself. I was on my way to find you. When I saw you dancing by yourself I said, I'll make a display of my doubts before Tiresias, and watch his reactions. He is old enough to be considered wise.

TIRESIAS (*preening*). Enough of that old Tiresias bit. Dionysos has knocked years off my back.

KADMOS. It's going round, it's catching Thebes on the rebound. Thebes has fallen out of love with our fossilised past and needs to embrace a new vitality. Come on, I am rearing to go.

TIRESIAS. Have you a crown?

KADMOS. Have I a crown? Ho ho. (*He reaches into a side-pouch and brings an ivy wreath. Sets it on his head at a rakish angle.*) If only you knew how my head has itched all day to put this on. Here, feel it. What do you think? Not too . . . dashing is it?

TIRESIAS. A bit fanciful for your age.

KADMOS. Now now, no more of that age nonsense. A man is as young as he feels and I feel thirty.

TIRESIAS. Well we'll just say you've set a new fashion then. Under divine inspiration.

KADMOS. Hey, have I told you about my daughters? They've got it really bad you know. They are all up in the mountains frisking around in the very madness of spring.

TIRESIAS. Ah yes, look around and see if those other women dropped bits of ivy while they were prancing about.

KADMOS. Yes, plenty around. What do you . . . ah of course. Hold on, I'll soon wreathe you a crown. (*Picks up a good bit of ivy and begins to weave a crown for* TIRESIAS.) What a relief to find one's innermost doubts banished once for all. What shall I do when I meet him Tiresias? He's my grandson after all, but still one must be careful with gods mustn't one?

TIRESIAS. Will you know him?

KADMOS. Why not? My own flesh and blood.

TIRESIAS. You've never seen him.

KADMOS. Doesn't matter. Flesh will call to flesh. I already sense his nearness.

TIRESIAS. Pentheus doesn't know his own flesh. And when he does he'll think he's duty-bound to cut it out of himself. If you held out the mirror of longing to him, he will utterly fail to recognise his own image or else he'll smash the mirror in anger.

KADMOS. There you go again talking in riddles. Here's your crown. Trad or trendy. (*He holds it poised over* TIRESIAS' *head.*)

TIRESIAS. We-e-e-ell, one is madness two is fashion. I don't like to see you mad.

KADMOS. Done. (*He stands some distance away and returns to adjust the angle.*) Perfect. Fawn-skin and ivy crowns. Oh Tiresias, do you think we've aged before our time?

TIRESIAS. You at least have lived, sower of dragon's teeth.

KADMOS. True. But then I wonder. Perhaps I retired too soon. It is wrong to wait for death isn't it. Simply to do nothing except wait for death. That's hardly a befitting end for a man. Suddenly I wonder about the past. From a life which constantly rejuvenated my bones I suddenly sat down and became an administrator. An administrator, Tiresias! Then an old-age pensioner on the Court List. I who slew the dragon and bred a race of warriors from his teeth.

TIRESIAS. It is good to rest sometimes.

KADMOS. Then will you tell me why suddenly I feel grape-skins under my feet?

TIRESIAS. Oh come let's go. Give me your hand.

KADMOS. Here hold on to me. Where shall we go? Where shall we tread this dance of life, tossing our white heads to the drums of Dionysos. Shall I lead the way to the mountains.

TIRESIAS. Lead the way.

KADMOS. I don't understand it. I am restless with a thousand schemes. Why should I keep thinking now I should never have left the throne to Pentheus? I know he will do something wrong. Shall I arrest him for his own good do you think? There are still soldiers loyal to me. We could stage a *coup d'état*.

TIRESIAS. To the mountains Kadmos. The god awaits us.

KADMOS. Ah well, maybe you're right. It is this new surge of life, I can't explain it. I feel I could even solve any of these riddles you are so fond of. I could dance all night without tiring, simply beating earth with my thyrsus. Hey, where is that anyway? (*He rummages inside his pouch and brings out a blunt-ended, telescoped object which he proceeds to pull out into a thyrsus. The following exchange is done music-hall style.*) Oh, what a shame you can't see to admire this Tiresias. Here, hold it in both hands, one hand at each end – that's it. Now pull out slowly. See how it works? First collapsible thyrsus in Attica, in the whole world maybe. Made it myself. Couldn't trust the palace joiner not to talk. Shows you how nervous I was, going all that length to disguise the obvious. (*Plants it on the ground meaning to use it as a walking stick. It collapses and he falls.* TIRESIAS *helps him up.*) The damned thing collapsed.

TIRESIAS. You can't expect it to be as strong as the joiner's.

KADMOS (*straightens it out*). Why not? It works doesn't it. Forgot to put a lock on it that's all. (*The thyrsus collapses again.*) Damn!

TIRESIAS (*as it fails again*). No good?

KADMOS. I can't walk through the streets with this. Let's go up in my chariot.

TIRESIAS. Walking is better. It shows more honour to the god.

KADMOS. With the shortest thyrsus in Thebes? I'll be a laughing-stock.

TIRESIAS. Let's go. Put it back in your trousers.

KADMOS (*morosely replacing it in the pouch*). I should have let the joiner show me how. But it could only make him cocky. (*They guffaw.*)

TIRESIAS. Where is your hand? When you step into the dance you'll lose all your silly notions. You accept, and that's the real stature of man. You are immersed in the richest essence of all – your inner essence. This is what the dance of Dionysos brings forth from you, this is the meaning of the dance. Follow the motion of my feet and dance Kadmos. We will dance all the way to the hills. One – Two – Back, One – Two – Back.

KADMOS (*obeys him*). I am a man, nothing more. I do not scoff at the will of heaven.

TIRESIAS. No, only fools trifle with divinity. People will say, Aren't you ashamed? At your age, dancing, wreathing your head with ivy? . . . Have you caught it? One – Two – Back, One – Two – Back.

KADMOS. I am not ashamed. Damn them, did the god declare that only the young or women must dance? They mean to kill us off before our time.

TIRESIAS. He has broken the barrier of age, the barrier of sex or slave and master. It is the will of Dionysos that no one be excluded from his worship.

KADMOS. Except those who exclude themselves. Like this one who approaches us, Tiresias. (*He stops dancing, makes* TIRESIAS *stop.*)

TIRESIAS. Who is it?

KADMOS. The man to whom I left the throne. He seems excited and disturbed. Let us keep out of his way for a while.

Enter PENTHEUS, *straight, militaristic in bearing and speech. His attendants have to run to keep up with him. Once on stage he strides angrily up and down.*

PENTHEUS.

    I shall have order! Let the city know at once
    Pentheus is here to give back order and sanity.
    To think those reports which came to be abroad are true!
    Not padded or strained. Disgustingly true in detail.
    If anything reality beggars the report. It's *disgusting*!
    I leave the country, I'm away only a moment
    Campaigning to secure our national frontiers. And what
        happens?
    Behind me – chaos! The city in uproar. Well, let everyone
    Know I've returned to re-impose order. Order!
    And tell it to the women especially, those
    Promiscuous bearers of this new disease.
    They leave their home, desert their children
    Follow the new fashion and join the Bacchae
    Flee the hearth to mob the mountains – those contain
    Deep shadows of course, secret caves to hide
    Lewd games for this new god – Dionysos!
    That's the holy spirit newly discovered.
    Dionysos! Their ecstasy is flooded down
    In brimming bowls of wine – so much for piety!
    Soused, with all the senses roused, they crawl
    Into the bushes and there of course a man
    Awaits them. All part of the service for this
    Mysterious deity. The hypocrisy? All they care about
    Is getting serviced. We netted a few.
    The rest have escaped into the mountains. I want them
    Hunted down. Chained and caged behind bars of iron.
    I want an end to the drunken dancing
    The filth, the orgies, the rot and creeping
    Poison in the body of state. I want Order and –
    I want immediate results. Go!

An OFFICER *salutes and exits.*

    And this stranger, who is he? A sorcerer?

Hypnotist? Some such kind of faker I'm sure, vomited
From Lydia, or Media, those decadent lands where
They wear their hair ribboned and curled,
Stink of scent and their cheeks are perpetually
Flushed with wine, their eyes full of furtive
Messages. So goes the report on this intruder.
The charlatan spends his days and nights only
In the company of our women. Calls it initiation.
I'll initiate his balls from his thighs once
We have him safely bound. I'll initiate
That head away from his body. I'll end his
Thumping, jumping, hair-tossing snaking game.
He claims Dionysos still lives? Some nerve!
A likely story for a brat who got roasted
Right in his mother's womb, blasted by the bolts
Of Zeus. The slut! Slandered Zeus by proclaiming
The bastard's divine paternity. That myth he instantly
Exploded in her womb, a fiery warning against all profanity.
You'd think my own relations would have learnt
From that family history but no! Ino and Autonoe
My own mother Agave are principals at the obscenities!
I'll teach them myself. I have woven
Iron nets to trap them. I'll bring an end
To the cunning subversion . . .

He sees TIRESIAS *and* KADMOS *for the first time.*

No . . . it's not true!
I won't believe it. Tiresias, seer of Thebes
Tricked out in a dappled fawn-skin? No.
And you, my own grandfather, surely not you!
Not playing at Bacchant with wand and ivy!
How awful to witness such foolishness in age.
Oh you disgust me, you, playing with infant toys.
I beg you now, shake off that ivy, drop
The wand of shame. Drop it I say!

He wheels back on TIRESIAS.

This is your doing Tiresias; I know
You talked him into it, and I know why.
Another god revealed is a new way opened
Into men's pockets, profits from offerings.
Power over private lives – and state affairs –
Don't deny it! I've known your busy priesthood
Manipulations. You try all you can, cleverly
To influence matters which belong to better trained
Heads than yours. It's all read in the entrails
Of fowls and goats of course. A new god!
Soon we'll have state policies revealed
In brimming cups of wine – by heaven! –
If you were not such a mouldering old ruin
You'd soon be rattling chains with others
Caged for smuggling in this lecherous gospel.
I warn you, presume too far on that protection and
I'll convince you Thebes is wide awake.
Thebes shall stop at nothing to preserve her good name
Faded with anarchy and indecency.

KADMOS.

Do not blaspheme, son. Have some respect
For heaven. Or at least for your elders.
I am still Kadmos, I sowed the dragon's teeth
And brought forth a race of supermen.
You are born of earth yourself – remember that.
Will the son of Ichion now disgrace his house?

TIRESIAS.

Oh it's so easy for some to make speeches.
They pick a soft target and the words rush out.
Now listen you. Your tongue runs loose
Makes a plausible sound and might
Almost be taken for sense. But you have none.
Your glibness flows from sheer conceit.

Arrogant, over-confident and a gift – yes –
A gift for phrases, and that makes you a great
Danger to your fellow men. For your mind
Is closed. Dead. Imprisoned in words.
    A new life
Comes into our midst, so vast, so potent
Soon it will be powerful all over Greece, but
You cannot feel it. Wake up Pentheus, open your heart.
Shall I tell you what to look for in this being?
Think of two principles, two supreme
Principles in life. First, the principle
Of earth, Demeter, goddess of soil or what you will.
This nourishes man, yields him grain. Bread. Womb-like
It earths him as it were, anchors his feet.
Second, the opposite, *and* complementary principle –
Ether, locked in the grape until released by man.
For after Demeter came the son of Semele
And matched her present with the juice of grapes.
Think of it as more than drug for pain
Though it is that. We wash our souls, our parched
Aching souls in streams of wine and enter
Sleep and oblivion. Filled with this good gift
Mankind forgets its grief. But wine is more!
It is the sun that comes after winter, the power
That nudges earth awake. Dionysos comes alive in us.
We soar, we fly, we shed the heavy clods of earth
That weigh down the ethereal man.
To that first principle. Balance is the key.
Now take this answer for your smear of bastardy
Though Dionysos needs no advocate. Too soon alas
You'll find that he can speak – and act – on his own behalf.
You ridicule the story men commonly repeat, that
This god was sewn into the thigh of Zeus?
Why do men quibble and clutch the literal for the sense?
If I should say to you Pentheus, you sprang from the loins

Of Kadmos here, full-formed, even to the teeth you so
Irreverently snap at me, what would it mean? Is the man
Not fully present in the seed? And the offspring
Of the son of Ichion, are they not even now esconced
Within that dangling pouch between your thighs?
Offsprings whose genesis you now endanger
By a sharp tongue wagging impiously?
It's not for me to say if Zeus had his scrotum
Sewn to one side of his thighs or
In-between like – presumably – yours.
Let's leave mythology aside. Think only of
And come to terms with what we know.

PENTHEUS.

And what do we know – apart from your casuistry?

TIRESIAS.

Our mortal condition, made of those two principles.

PENTHEUS.

I said, apart from your quibbling.

TIRESIAS.

Use your eyes Pentheus. I cannot see but I do
Know. And feel. And so do you, though you will not
Accept. You see this power made manifest
Yet you deny it. Think again of human fate –
What is this but a journey towards death.
Extinction. But visions open up another world, give
Strength and consolation. Through Dionysos we
Transcend that putrefaction of the flesh that begins
From the instant of our drawing breath.
This is a god of prophecy. His worshippers
Like seers, are endowed with mantic powers.
Reason is cluttered by too much matter-details,
Cravings, acquisitions, anxieties. When he invades the mind
Reason is put to sleep. He frees the mind
Expands and fills it with uplifting visions.
Flesh is transcended. What else? Where else?

At war you'll find him, confounding the enemy
With the unnatural courage of his followers.
And at Delphi too, home of Apollo, sanctuary
Of reason. How else does the priestess enter
The oracular state?

PENTHEUS (*angry*).

That's blasphemy!

TIRESIAS.

Slander perhaps, or heresy. A priestess is no god.
You are the blasphemer.

PENTHEUS.

I warn you. . . .

TIRESIAS.

Is it not customary to pour libations
At the altar of Apollo? This is
To pour the body of god itself and through
His intercession win the favour of heaven.

PENTHEUS.

You are quibbling again, you are trying
To wriggle out of the smear you laid upon
Apollo's priesthood.

TIRESIAS.

What Apollo does not reject cannot harm
His servant. A drop for the altar, the rest
To smooth the passage of prayers up the throat.

PENTHEUS.

You go too far Tiresias!

TIRESIAS.

Not so far as Dionysos means to go. Oh
Accept him Pentheus. Look up at the rockhills.
Whom do you see bounding
Over the high plateau through needle peaks
Whose is the rustle of wind in pine forests
Shaking winter into life with green branches?
Dionysos is here

In your state. He is at work
All over the world.
Accept him
Pour wine for him
Put vine leaves in your hair for him
Dance for him.

PENTHEUS.

You would love that. Madness and folly
Ever seek company. Licentiousness requires
The stamp of approval from a head of state
To break the last barriers of restraint.
Then power passes into the hands of those
Who prove the most self-abandoned.

TIRESIAS.

If only you would lose this notion that power
Is all that matters in the life of man.
Do not mistake for wisdom these fantasies
Of your sick mind. Abandonment? Dionysos, I admit
Will not restrain desire in man or woman.
Yet if a woman is chaste in nature she stays
Uncorrupted in the rites of Dionysos.
Restraint is something people must practise
Themselves. It cannot be imposed. Those
Who have learnt self-discipline – the greatest
Guarantee of human will and freedom –
Will not then lose it for losing themselves
To Dionysos. Answer me, is control not built
Upon self-knowledge?

PENTHEUS.

What if it is?

TIRESIAS.

Dionysos grants self-knowledge. With that thought
I leave you. There is still time.
Save yourself if you can; look inwards, ask –
Does Pentheus truly know himself?

KADMOS.

>Son, you are pleased to have men crowd
>Around the city gates to welcome you,
>And every street rings with the name –
>'Pentheus! Pentheus!' A god deserves no less.

TIRESIAS.

>Come, we have done our duty.
>We shall dance you and I, partner each other
>An ancient foolish pair perhaps, but – dance we must
>Not fight this power. I pity Pentheus
>His terrible madness. There is no cure,
>No relief from potions. Nor from preaching.

KADMOS.

>Wait. His mind is surely distracted,
>His thoughts sheer delirium. – Son, remember
>That dreadful death your cousin Actaeon died
>When those man-eating hounds reared
>By his own hands savaged him, tore him
>Limb from limb for boasting that his prowess
>In the hunt surpassed the skill of Artemis.
>Do not let his fate be yours.

PENTHEUS (*grimly*).

>It won't. But I thank you for suggesting a most
>Befitting fate for that sorcerer when we find him.

KADMOS.

>Not sorcerer. God. And even if your mind
>Will not accept his person – I know appearances
>Do more than prejudice even men of reason –
>Since you must know within yourself, secretly
>In the silence of your heart, this force *exists*
>Take him simply as high priest of the rites and
>Semele is at least mother of a seer
>Conferring great distinction on our family.

Misjudging the thoughtful distant mood of PENTHEUS, *he thinks he has at least mollified his stand. He removes the wreath from his own head.*

KADMOS.

> Here, take mine. Let me wreathe
> Your head with leaves of ivy. Come with us,
> Glorify the god!

PENTHEUS (*knocks it off*).

> Take your hands off me! Get out!
> Go and play Bacchae, but don't wipe
> Your drooling idiocy off on me. Don't you dare
> Touch our person again. As for you Tiresias
> Your punishment need not wait.
> One moment longer. I'll make you pay
> Dearly for this folly of yours. (*Turns to his attendants.*)
> > Go, this instant!
> Find the place where this prophet sits
> Faking revelations out of birdsong. Go.
> Pry it up with crowbars, heave it over
> Upside down. Demolish everything you see.
> Throw his fillets out to wind and weather.
> That will teach you! The rest of you,
> Go scour the city, bring me this foreigner
> This thing of doubtful gender who infects
> Our women with his strange disease and pollutes
> Our marriage beds. Find him. Clap him in chains.
> Drag him here. He'll suffer stoning to death
> The nearest fate I can devise to Acteon's
> Piecemeal death at the jaws of his hunting hounds.
> He'll find Thebes a harder bed than he had
> Bargained for his Bacchic jigs.

The attendants hesitate. They move as far as the exit, stop.

TIRESIAS.

> You are mad. Do you realise what you're saying?

You made little enough sense before but now –
You are raving! Lead me out of here Kadmos.
It's almost an impiety to stay beside such folly.
We must no longer think of him, only of us.
Pray that for the sake of Thebes, this folly
Is overlooked. We must harness this great force
For our common good.

As they exit.

Kadmos, in Greek the name Pentheus signifies
Sorrow. Does that mean anything? Let's hope not.

PENTHEUS (*turns round, attracted by whispering. He is surprised to see his attendants still there*). Are you still here?

OLD SLAVE *comes forward.*

OLD SLAVE. We wondered . . . about the hut of the holy man . . . you would not . . . really want it destroyed?

For reply PENTHEUS *fetches him a slap which knocks him flat.*

PENTHEUS. Slave! Is that language simple enough even for a slave? Something is wrong with the old men of this city. It affects freemen and slaves alike.

SLAVE LEADER.
Back! Keep back!

VARIOUS.
– Keep away!
– This is filth, stain
– Smear, decay.
– Abomination

SLAVE LEADER.
Back! Leave him there
Let him lie there and accuse him!

VARIOUS.
– With the scorn that dripped
Scathing, corroding from his mouth

Fouling Dionysos, child of his own city.
– I am a stranger, but I think
Now I know Dionysos.

PENTHEUS (*his hand on his sword*).
Do you slaves defy me?

VARIOUS.
We are strangers but we know the meaning of madness
– To hit an old servant
With frost on his head
Such a one as has stood
At the gateway of Mysteries.

SLAVE LEADER.
You know it. This
Was the body of the Old Year Dying
The choice of the priests of Eleusis
Till good Tiresias stepped in his place.

SLAVE.
And now you'll pull down the Old Seer's hut.

SLAVE LEADER.
You said to the Master of Revels
Take him – Perhaps he'll live, or the gods
Will claim him – he's old enough.
Is such a one to be violated by you?

VARIOUS.
Oh the scorn on his lips. Such
Inhuman indifference. Corrosive
As his hate for Dionysos.
–   Age is holy
To hit an old man
Or demolish the roof of a sage?
–   Yet we are the barbarians
And Greece the boast of civilisation.
We are slaves and have no souls.

SLAVE LEADER.
No one will touch him where he lies

The world must see it.
Dionysos shall avenge this profanity
I live to witness
The feast of the vengeance of joy. O-oh
I have heard earth turn at the tramp
Of dancing Bacchantes and, my heart
Has leapt. At the sound of flutes, whole
Galaxies have fallen in my cupped hands
I have drunk the stars. . . .

He bows his head suddenly and intones, the others repeating each line after him, as if this is a practised liturgy. PENTHEUS' *face registers horror and disbelief as he recognises the implications of this.*

And yielded to the power of life, the god in me
To the seminal flood that courses earth and me
The alliance of blood to wine, the bond
Of ether and flesh, earth, and the breath in me.
And this is what this day we celebrate
Our feet at the dance are the feet of men
Grape-pressing, grain-winnowing, our joy
Is the great joy of union with mother earth
And the end of separation between man and man.

SLAVE LEADER (*alone*).
Said Bromius,
I am the gentle comb of breezes on the slope of vines
The autumn flush on clustered joy of grapes
I am the autumn sacrament, the bond, word, pledge
The blood rejuvenated from a dying world
I am the life that's trodden by the dance of joy
My flesh, my death, my re-birth is the song
That rises from men's lips, they know not how.
But also,
The wild blood of the predator that's held in leash
The fearful flames that prowl the thicket of the night
I melt as wax the wilful barriers of human mind
Gently even in this, except to the tyrant mind

That thinks to damn the flood-tide from the hills.
I am Dionysos. (*A pause of an instant, then, powerfully.*)
    Lead us Bromius!

SLAVES. Lead us –!

PENTHEUS (*he has snatched out his sword*). Shut up! (*Dead silence.*)
I'll cut out the tongue of the next man to utter that name
Bromius or Dionysos!

Enter DIONYSOS, *captive, surrounded by soldiers. Three or four*
BACCHANTES *are with him, their hands similarly tied.*

DIONYSOS. Who calls on Dionysos! You, Pentheus?

There is a dead freeze of several moments.* PENTHEUS *moves first,*
approaches the prisoner and inspects him in silence. The OFFICER
begins his report, PENTHEUS *continues his inspection.*

OFFICER.
    We found him Pentheus. The hunt is over
    Here is the animal you sent us after.
    And not so dangerous after all, quite docile
    To tell the truth. We had no trouble over him,
    Handed himself over without a murmur
    Held out his arms for the chains, no attempt
    To run or hide, or escape our dragnet.
    To confess the truth, that bothered me.
    I was – well – quite embarrassed. It seemed
    Not quite playing the game. For a professional –
    Code of conflict and all that – well – I felt
    Quite ashamed. I said to him, Stranger,
    I am not here by choice. I take orders and
    My orders were to bring you live to Pentheus.
    He seemed to understand. Oh, another thing.
    The women you locked up in gaol are free.
    They've shed their chains, they're up away
    In the forests and mountains, running like deer,

* The Interval, if any, should take place here, the second half remaining
from the same positions.

Calling on their god Bromius. He seems to be
Their master, governs them completely.
Naturally, I probed the matter. I am
Compelled to report the truth. It was no
Human hands that snapped those chains, no
Human cunning picked the locks on those
Iron gates. The thing is beyond me. Thebes
Is suddenly full of miracles – I say no more.
The rest is your affair.

PENTHEUS.
Untie his hands. He is fast within our net
And cannot escape.

They untie him. DIONYSOS *and* PENTHEUS *stand face to face.*

So. You are not at all bad-looking
Quite attractive I am sure, to women.
Perhaps it was this that brought you to Thebes –
Our women have a reputation for being easy game. . . .
Long hair, all nicely curled. Hold out your hands.

DIONYSOS *obeys.*

I thought so. You have never wrestled
Or done a day's work in the fields. The arts
Of war must be just as strange to you. Your skin
Is smooth. You cultivate the shadows, the dark
For the larks of Aphrodite. Ah yes,
And what they call a handsome profile, quite
An asset in your style of life. Now answer straight:
Who are you? Where do you come from?

DIONYSOS.
I am . . .
Nothing of note, nothing to boast of.
As for where – have you heard of a river
Called Tmolus. It runs
Through fields of flowers.

PENTHEUS.

Yes, I know that river.

It circles the city of Sardis.

DIONYSOS.

I come from there.

My country is Lydia.

PENTHEUS.

Hm, that fits with my reports.

And who is this new god whose worship

You have brought to us in Hellas?

DIONYSOS.

Dionysos, the son of Zeus. The god himself

Initiated me.

PENTHEUS.

You have some local Zeus there

Who spawns new gods?

DIONYSOS.

He is the same as yours.

The Zeus who sowed his seed

In earth.

PENTHEUS.

And he initiated you. Was it

In truth-defining day, or was it by night

This 'inspiration' came to you.

DIONYSOS.

Will you reduce it all to a court

Of enquiry? A fact-finding commission such as

One might set up to decide the cause

Of a revolt in your salt-mines, or a slave uprising?

These matters are beyond the routine machinery of state.

PENTHEUS.

Answer me!

DIONYSOS.

How does the earth take seed? By night

Or day? When heaven opens forth and
Swarms and probes earth's thirsty womb, do you ask
Did her 'inspiration' come by night or day?
And when the grape begins to swell, its red juice
Pounding on the tender skin or, at the sight
Of the bursting udder of a cow
Do you wait to date and time
Her 'inspiration' or simply fetch the milk-pail?
Do you demand of earth the secret of the vine or
Tread the grapes and say a prayer of thanks to heaven?

PENTHEUS.
So it is all, and must remain a secret?

DIONYSOS.
To those in whom Dionysos is not born.
To others there are no secrets for
Their minds are open.

PENTHEUS.
You are clever, but not clever enough.
If there were no shameful acts in this
New worship, you would hardly wait to speak.

DIONYSOS.
Mysteries are only for the initiates.
And in this worship all, even you Pentheus
May enter into the mysteries.

PENTHEUS.
Very clever. Your answers are designed
To make me curious. Tell me this at least
What benefits do the initiates derive,
The followers of this god?

DIONYSOS.
Again I am forbidden to say. But they are
Well worth knowing.

PENTHEUS.
I see your game, it is so transparent.
You think to play on my curiosity.

DIONYSOS.

Our Mysteries abhor an unbelieving man.

PENTHEUS.

You say you saw the god? What form
Did he assume?

DIONYSOS.

The form of all men, all beasts
And all nature. He chose at will.

PENTHEUS.

You evade my question.

DIONYSOS.

Talk truth to a deaf man and he
Begs your pardon.

PENTHEUS.

You grow bold, stranger. In a moment
You shall learn how unwise that is.
Now, are we the first to suffer your visitation
Or have you spread your dirt in other cities?

DIONYSOS.

The world everywhere now dances for Dionysos.

PENTHEUS.

We have more sense than barbarians.
Greece has a culture.

DIONYSOS.

Just how much have you travelled Pentheus?
I have seen even among your so-called
Barbarian slaves natives of lands whose cultures
Beggar yours.

PENTHEUS.

Don't try to wander off the subject.
These sacred practices of your god, the worship
The rites of great devotion, do they
Hold at night, or in the day?

DIONYSOS (*kindly, very gently and without scorn or attack*).

Poor Pentheus, how you must suffer, tying

So rigidly the hour of day and night with sin or virtue.
We hold our rites mostly at night, but only
Because it is cooler. And the lamps
Lend atmosphere and feeling to the heart in worship.
The lighting of a lamp is in itself
A votive act. Oil is an offering. A woman
Bears a lamp and the ring of light that falls
Around her frame is magic, holy,
A secretive and tender kind of grace. Think of a dark
   mountain
Pierced by myriads of tiny flames, then see
The human mind as that dark mountain whose caves
Are filled with self-inflicted fears. Dionysos
Is the flame that puts such fears to flight, a flame
That must be gently lit, or else consume you.

PENTHEUS (*violently*).
And I say night hours are dangerous
Lascivious hours, lechery. . . .

DIONYSOS.
You'll find debauchery in daylight too.

PENTHEUS.
You wrestle well – with words. You will regret
Your ill-timed cleverness.

DIONYSOS (*wearily*).
And you, your stupid blasphemies.

PENTHEUS.
Enough! You, bring me the shears!

DIONYSOS.
Shears? What terrible fate am I to undergo?

PENTHEUS.
First, we shall rid you of your girlish curls.

DIONYSOS.
My hair is holy. My curls belong to god.

PENTHEUS *shears off his hair.*

PENTHEUS.

Next, you will surrender the wand.

DIONYSOS.

You will have to take it. It belongs
To Dionysos.

PENTHEUS (*snatching it*).

You think I fear a common
Conjurer's wand? And now we will place you
Under guard and confine you to the palace.

DIONYSOS.

Dionysos will set me free whenever I request it.

PENTHEUS.

Yes, when you get your followers round you
And 'summon his presence'!

DIONYSOS.

He sees. He is here. This minute he knows
What is being done to me.

PENTHEUS.

Where is he then? Is he always invisible?
Why doesn't he show himself?

DIONYSOS.

He does, but you being crass and insensitive
You can see nothing.

PENTHEUS.

You insult me? You must be raving!

To the GUARDS.

He insults your king. He insults Thebes.
Load him with chains! The man is insane.

DIONYSOS.

I am sane, but you are not. I warn you,
Set me free.

PENTHEUS.

Chain him I say! Weight him down with chains.
I'll show you who has the power here.

DIONYSOS.

> You do not know what life is. You do not know
> What you do. You do not know the limits
> Of your power. You will not be forgiven.

PENTHEUS.

> What are you all waiting for. Chain him I said.

The GUARDS *with obvious reluctance approach him with chains.*

DIONYSOS.

> I give you sober warning Pentheus.
> Place no chains on me.

The GUARDS *chain him quickly, move away as if from a distasteful job.*

PENTHEUS.

> I am Pentheus, son of Ichion.
> You are – nothing.

DIONYSOS.

> Pentheus. The name befits a doomed man.

PENTHEUS.

> Oh take him away. Get him out of my sight.
> He talks and talks. Lock him up somewhere near –
> In the stables – yes, leave him in the stables
> Let him thrash in the hay and light up his darkness
> With the flame of Dionysos. Dance in there.
> And the creatures you brought with you, your
> Accomplices in subversion, I shall have them
> Sold to slavery. They'll work in mines or carry
> Water for the troops, day and night – that
> Will silence their drums. (*Exit* PENTHEUS.)

As DIONYSOS *is chained, his* BACCHANTES *begin a noise, a kind of ululating which is found among some African and Oriental peoples and signifies great distress, warning, or agitation. Sometimes all combined. It increases in volume. As* DIONYSOS *is led away it spreads towards the* SLAVE CHORUS *swelling into deafening proportions.*

DIONYSOS.

> I leave you now. I go, not to suffer
> For that cannot be. But Dionysos whose
> Godhead you deny will call you to account.
> When you set chains on me, you manacle the god.

From within the shrieking intensity of sound protesting the sacrilege,
a BACCHANTE'*s voice rises.*

BACCHANTE.

> He rages. He is full of the mad wind
> Of rage. Pentheus, son of Ichion and Agave
> I know now you are mad. You have chained
> The messenger of god.

SLAVE

> Why am I rejected? Why am I a second time
> Rejected O blessed Tmolus. First, banished
> From your banks into this city, a slave. And now to see
> The promise broken, the messenger of Bromius in chains
> Heavier than mine! Rejected? Pentheus!
> By the clustered grapes on the hills I swear
> You shall come to know the name of Bromius!

BACCHANTE.

> He, a second time rejected, sweet Dirce
> Life-stream to these fields! Again
> Rejected from your sweet breast, from
> Banks that were a cradle for the new-born child.

ANOTHER.

> I heard the voice of Zeus in thunder
> Saying, Welcome my son,
> Welcome to the world, spirit of all
> That lives and moves. . . .

SLAVE.

> Free spirit, soul of liberty, seed of the new order.

BACCHANTE.

> Yet this river spurns the god a second time!

Come not near. No ivy crowns on my banks
No gatherings, no dances, no flutes
To ruffle flowers on my bank.

ANOTHER.

Oh some day you'll thirst, ache
Parched, long for this immortal
Communion.
Yes, some day, you'll crave
Dionysos.

SLAVE.

Such fury from his eyes, yet not he
Violated, outraged. But the fury!
With rage, with fury he rages. No, not a man.
A beast run wild. A crop of dragon's teeth
That earth has never tamed with nursing.
A freak, a monster
Gorged and rank with pestilence. . . .

BACCHANTE.

A fiend, murderous to the bone. And this,
This thing means to shut me up, to
Plunge me in the darkness of his mind!
I am not his. I belong
To Dionysos!

ANOTHER.

In a dungeon, in a sightless pit
He buries our leader.

OLD SLAVE.

He is nothing. A trickster. Windbag. A commonplace
Illusionist. Beyond that, nothing.
Briefly I dreamt I saw salvation. Now
The breeder of false cravings lies
Bound in the net of his own spinning
Crushed.

FIRST BACCHANTE.

CRUSHED?

SEVERAL.

>NO! NO! NO!

FIRST BACCHANTE.

>Chained, but like a tower of gold.

BACCHANTE.

>A column of the sun that touches
>Earth from Olympios.

ALL.

>Come Dionysos!

BACCHANTE.

>With a tree in his hand, the rockhills
>Of his brow are drawn, they frown . . .

ANOTHER.

>Down on the palace walls of Pentheus –
>Come Dionysos!

SLAVE LEADER.

>Pentheus! Retribution lowers
>From the brow of a prisoner.

SLAVES.

>Come Dionysos!

SLAVE LEADER.

>Prestidigitator god

FIRST BACCHANTE.

>Apocalyptic utterance

SLAVE LEADER.

>Bromius, come, COME! Be manifest!

VARIOUS.

- Come from the mountain forests
- Glide from the wild beast's lair
- Spring from a cruel peak
- Leap from a whirlwind dance
- Burst from a thousand oaks
- Rise from the silent valley
  A tree-leaved menace
  Like the end of Orpheus' spell

On the hounds of death
- Breaking the forest netting
On limbs of mahogany
- From out of mountain torrents
Heralded on drumming feet
- Surge over waves towards us
Over green plains, a raging stallion

SLAVE.
Break interminable shackles
Break bonds of oppressors
Break the beast of blood
Break bars that sprout
In travesty of growth

FIRST BACCHANTE.
Wounding the farmlands
Bruising the grapes
Lashing the late buds
Ploughing the hills
Watering the fields
In torrents of wine
Spirit of motion
Quickener of life
Oh let your sweet grape burst in me
Come Dionysos!

ALL (ecstatically).
Bromius! Bromius! BROMIUS!

A loud rumble, as of thunder. A hush falls on the scene.

FIRST BACCHANTE.
It is happening. Do you hear it?
I know it is happening.

CHORUS (a whisper).
Bromius?

FIRST BACCHANTE.
It is happening. I hear him

In footsteps of the earthquake.

CHORUS.

Bromius?

FIRST BACCHANTE.

In the chords that Orpheus fingered
In the hunger of women

CHORUS.

Bromius?

FIRST BACCHANTE.

In the terror of children
And the anger of slaves.

CHORUS.

Now. Now is the time. Bromius
Be manifest! Come, the new order!

BACCHANTE.

Shatter the floor of the world!

SLAVE LEADER.

It's happening. The palace of Pentheus
Totters, bulges, quivers. Rot gapes
In the angry light of lightning. Roots
Long trapped in evil crevices have burgeoned
Their strength empowers me, the strength
Of a Master. . . . Join him! Power his will!

CHORUS.

Come BROMIUS!

Again, another rending as of deep thunder rolling off into a distance.
Like heavy breathing : In – Out.

FIRST BACCHANTE.

Earth –

CHORUS.

Shake!

FIRST BACCHANTE.

Earth –

CHORUS.
     Retch!
FIRST BACCHANTE.
     Earth –
CHORUS.
     Melt!
FIRST BACCHANTE.
     Earth –
CHORUS.
     Swarm!
FIRST BACCHANTE.
     Earth –
CHORUS.
     Take!
FIRST BACCHANTE.
     Earth –
CHORUS.
     Swell!
FIRST BACCHANTE.
     Earth –
CHORUS.
     Grow!
FIRST BACCHANTE.
     Earth –
CHORUS.
     Move!
FIRST BACCHANTE.
     Earth –
CHORUS.
     Strain!
FIRST BACCHANTE.
     Earth –
CHORUS.
     Groan!

FIRST BACCHANTE.

Earth –

CHORUS.

Clutch!

FIRST BACCHANTE.

Earth –

CHORUS.

Thrust!

FIRST BACCHANTE.

Earth –

CHORUS.

Burst!

FIRST BACCHANTE.

Earth –

CHORUS.

TAKE!

FIRST BACCHANTE.

Earth –

CHORUS.

Breathe! Live! Blow upon the walls of darkness.
Melt, marble, pillars, take! Take! TAKE!

FIRST BACCHANTE.

Adore him!

CHORUS.

We adore him.

Darkness, thunder, flames. Roar of collapsing masonry. From among it all, the music of DIONYSOS.

FIRST BACCHANTE.

Flames! The fevered flames around the grave
Of Semele, charred earth that no one walks upon
Except. . . .

DIONYSOS.

Dionysos.

He is revealed as first seen standing in the charred ruin of the grave of

Semele. The flames are higher round his feet. The BACCHANTES
and the CHORUS *are down on their faces.*

BACCHANTE.
    We do not move, or look, or breathe.
DIONYSOS.
    Afraid, my companions from distant lands?
    Look at you, hugging the earth, terror struck.
    You saw the house of darkness split and sundered –
    For Dionysos was there. You willed him,
    Summoned him, your needs
    Invoked his presence. Why do you tremble?
    Look up. Look up at me. The mortal ribs of Pentheus
    Crumble, sundered by the presence
    Of the eternal. Look up. All is well.
BACCHANTE.
    The dawn we know, our life-light departed
    When you left in chains.
DIONYSOS.
    Did you think I would be buried in those
    Death cells of Pentheus' darkness, and so
    Settle down to despair?
OLD SLAVE.
    You are free?
DIONYSOS.
    You willed my freedom, I could not resist.
SLAVE.
    How did you do it? How did you escape?
DIONYSOS.
    With ease. No effort was required.
SLAVE.
    With manacles on your wrists? That man
    Had blood-lust in his eyes.
DIONYSOS.
    Oh, but there I fooled him. It was my turn

To humiliate the godless fool, serve him
Outrage for outrage. I made the sick desires
Of his mind his goal, and he pursued them.
He fed on vapours of his own malignant
Hate, pursued and roped mirages in the stable,
Manacled hooves and horns of a docile bull,
Stumbled on pails, wrestled beams, lost his way
In collapsing hay, slipped on manure
Then sat in a lather of sweat, chewing his lips
Cursing the stranger from Phyrgia.
I sat nearby, quietly watching. Untouched.
That moment came Dionysos.
He shook the roof of the palace of Pentheus
Touched the living grave and cradle of his being
And up leapt ribbons of fire. Pentheus looked up
He saw – only his palace, possessions, his high estate
Menaced by passionate flames. From end to end
Of his palace he rushed, screaming at servants
To pour water, more water on water till every slave
Was working – over nothing. The fire existed
Only in his unquiet mind. He left it suddenly –
A fear had crept upon him that I might escape –
Snatched up a long steel sword and hurled himself
Back into the stables. His prisoner was gone,
But there was bright, gleaming air where Dionysos
Had been. At this emanation in the stable gloom
Pentheus charged, stabbing and lunging, thinking
To slake his vengeance in my blood. More folly.
And it brought more havoc in its wake. For now Dionysos
Razed the palace to the ground, reduced it
To utter ruins. At that bitter sight
Pentheus, spent and limp, threw away his sword
Broken by the struggle. Well, he is only a man
He exceeded himself, tried to fight a god.
Quietly I left the house, came back to you.

He never touched me.
                              Listen. I hear footsteps
That would be him. He'll come out and rave and swear . . .
But what can he say now? Let him bluster,
I'll manage him easily. The secret of life is
Balance, tolerance . . . perhaps he's learnt that now.

Enter PENTHEUS.

PENTHEUS.
    I had him trussed up. He could not move.
    Still, he got away. I have been tricked.

He sees DIONYSOS.

                                        What! You?
    How did you escape? Answer me!
DIONYSOS.
    Tread lightly. Let your anger drain off . . .
    Slowly . . . slowly. . . .
PENTHEUS (*even more peremptorily*).
    How did you escape?
DIONYSOS.
    Have you forgotten? Someone, I said
    Would set me free.
PENTHEUS.
    Who? Spell out his name.
DIONYSOS.
    He who tends the grape for mankind.
PENTHEUS.
    He who sows drunkenness and disorder!
DIONYSOS.
    Poor Pentheus. He has learnt nothing.
PENTHEUS (*to the* GUARDS).
    Surround the palace. Close every gate in the city.
    Seal up every nook and cranny. I want the city
    Bolted tight.

DIONYSOS.

You are truly incurable. These powers
That you dispute move on a higher plane
Than towers and city walls.

PENTHEUS.

Very clever talk, as usual. This time
It will not help you.

DIONYSOS.

No. I use it thinking to help *you*. As usual
It is futile. You are a doomed man Pentheus.
Look, here comes someone with a message.
Listen to him first. Carefully, don't hurry anything.
We are in no hurry. We'll wait for you.
Hear what he has to say; he comes from the mountains.

HERDSMAN.

Pentheus, I am one of your subjects here
In Thebes. I am just from Kithairon. The snow
Is there still and white hills dazzle you. . . .

PENTHEUS.

Get to the point man! What is your news?

HERDSMAN.

Sire, I have seen
Miracles. The very stuff of ballads. You cannot . . .
No, wait. If I must report faithfully . . .
You see, it has to do with the Maenads, those
Women who run barefoot from city to city . . .
I have witnessed weird, fantastic things, but . . .
Can I speak freely, and in my own way?
Master, you have a cruel temper. We, your subjects
Know it to our cost. And all too often.

PENTHEUS.

You may speak freely. Do your duty and nothing
Will happen to you. You have my promise.
Tell me the worst things they've done, the worse
It shall be for the man who began it.

But you are safe – speak.

HERDSMAN.

Well then – and may the god of oaths protect me –
Our herds of cattle had just climbed up a hill
Grazing as they went – the dew was wet upon the grass,
The sun being hardly warmed up at that early hour –
Well, by chance I stumble on this meadow, and in it
Find a scene just like a painting on a vase – motionless –
Three rings of women – fast sleep. One brief look
Is enough. I say to myself – it's *them*.
One is grouped round Autonoe – that would be your
Auntie I think. The second I was more sure of – Agave
Your mother. The third had to be Ino. Each ring
Is formed around the leader, in a kind of
Magic circle to my thinking. They were *still*,
So peaceful it seemed a shame they had to wake.
Some you'd find propped against the pine-tree trunks
Others, curled up on a pile of oak leaves
A few were simply pillowed on earth. I found there
None of that drunkenness we'd heard so much about,
None of the obscene abandon, or the wild music.
No topping among the bushes. If I may describe it –
A kind of radiant peace, like the sacred grove of a deity.
Well, our cattle soon put an end to that. Their lowing
Wakes up your mother, she leaps up, cries out
And wakes the rest of the women. Her voice was clear
And strangely tuneful in those echoing hills. I heard her
Warn the others, men and cattle were close by.
They shook off sleep from their eyes, yet even awake
That air of peace still controlled their actions . . .
And such beauties! We do have some treasures in Thebes.
Young supple limbs, maidens who have yet to know man –
Such jet and gold flew through the air when they let fall
Their hair. They brushed their clothes, then
Fastened them at the waist with . . . well, tell me I'm lying –

Snakes! *Live* snakes! I see their tongues still flickering
Clearly as I see you now! But that was nothing.
There was still more live wonder to come.
Have you ever seen a woman nurse a fawn
Exactly like a child? Or a wild wolf cub? I mean
To the point where she gives it suck? From – her – own –
    breast!
Heavy of breast those were, newly delivered,
Left their own babes at home – you know, the breast
Can get painful with milk – but to suckle a wild cub!
Again, that is nothing, for now rushed one miracle
After another. From weaving strands of ivy,
Oak-leaves, and flowering bryony to dress their hair,
One turned to twining leaves around a branch and,
Like the most natural act you could conceive, she
Tapped a rock and – tell me I'm lying – out of that rock
Spouts – water! Clear, spring water, fresh as dew.
Another drove her fennel in the ground and, where
The earth was wounded – another spring! But this time –
Wine! A wine-spring! Two women on their knees
Scrape the soil with fingers and out flows
Milk, creamier than the morning yield from a champion cow.
From all their ivy-covered branches, sweet honey
Dripped in golden cascades . . . oh sire, if you had been there
If you had witnessed but a part you would be
On bended knees, giving thanks, praying the heavens
For help and guidance.
                            We met, shepherds and cowherds
Gathered in small groups to argue, comparing rumours
With this real event, for these were fantastic
Deeds! We could hardly believe our eyes. Now,
Up gets a city fellow, a great one for speeches,
Seizes his chance and addresses our group:
'Friends from the meadows of these mountains' –
Majestic meadows he said – I'll give him his due –

'Allow me to suggest a judicious and expedient hunt
One not without great expectations. Let us pursue
Agave the Queen-mother, rescue and bear her from these
Unmajestic orgiastics. Indubitably I declare
Pentheus will most royally reward us.' That did it.
Who would turn his back on such a business? Straightway we
Devised an ambush for the women. We hid
Among the undergrowth covered in leaves. We waited.
The hour for their ritual soon approached
Their ivy-covered staves were beating earth in rhythm –
It gets in your blood, that rhythm, it really does –
The chanting began – 'Iacchos' 'Dionysos'
'Bromius!' 'Son of Zeus!'
                              Everything
The very mountain seemed to sway to that one beat
A beat like the hearts of a thousand men in unison.
The beasts moved with them, they seemed
Touched by a savage divinity.

                              It quickened.
The Maenads were swift upon their feet, rapt, unseeing,
Blind to all except the vision of their god.
Agave raced towards me, she flew close
Her arms were flashing like blades but I leapt,
My hands hot on the quarry. That scream!
I never will forget that screaming summons from her lips
To her swift hounds – for so she termed them –
Exhorting them to follow and turn hunter.
And they obeyed her. We changed roles and became the
     hunted.
Fleeing for sweet life. Another moment and
We would have been shredded like chaff.
Balked of their prey, the Maenads turned upon our herd.
Unarmed, they swooped down on our heifers grazing
In the meadows, nothing in their hands, nothing.
Their bare arms sufficed. They rent young, stocky

Heifers in two – you should have heard their death bellows,
Seen these frail-built creatures wrench
Full-grown cattle limb from limb, ribs, hooves
Spiral in the air, fall in torrents of blood,
Seen our dismembered livestock hang from branches
Blood spattering the leaves, seen wild bulls
With surging horns, unapproachable till now
Tripped, sprawled full-length on the ground
Bellow in unaccustomed terror as girlish limbs
Tore them apart, flayed them living.
There was a force within them; it drove them
Uphill, their feet hardly touching the ground.
Like invaders they swooped into Hysiae
Sacked Erythrae in the foothills of Kithairon.
Nothing withstood them, they pillaged and raided
Snatched children from homes, razed walls to the ground.
And all this plunder they piled upon their backs.
Nothing held it, nothing. Yet neither bronze nor iron
Fell to the ground. Flames flickered in their curls but
Their hair remained unsinged.

Until at last,

Mad at these monstrosities, some villagers
Foolishly took to arms and made to attack them.
It was a terrible sight my masters. The men's
Spears and swords are lethal and sharp but,
They draw no blood, while the wands of the women . . .!
The men ran, yes, *ran*! Routed by women!
Master, it is not for me to say, but
Some god was surely with them. I watched them
Transformed in an instant, troop peacefully back
To where they had started, by those springs magically
Bestowed by their god, wash stains from their bodies
And the snakes licking the drops of blood
That clung to their hair.

Whoever this god may be

Sire, welcome him to Thebes. He is great
In other ways I hear. Didn't he make us
Mortal men the gift of wine? If that is true
You have much to thank him for – wine makes
Our labours bearable. Take wine away
And the world is without joy, tolerance or love.

PENTHEUS *remains as he is for some moments.*

PENTHEUS.
It spreads, the craze, the violence,
Like a blazing fire. It comes close, close,
It comes too close. It contaminates even by report.
As a people we are disgraced, humiliated.
It's firmness now, no more hesitation.

To the OFFICER.

Go to the gates of Electra, order out
All the heavy-armoured infantry.
Call out the fastest troops of the cavalry
The mobile squadrons and the archers.
Issue a general call-up – all able-bodied men
Who can hold shield and spear. Set in motion
The standard drill for a state of emergency –
I have reasons for that – these restive dogs
Might see their chance to stage a slave uprising,
I have seen signs, so see to it!
I want the troops massed here directly.
We attack the Bacchae at once.

DIONYSOS.
Pentheus . . .

PENTHEUS. Shut up! (*Turns to a* GUARD.) You. Give me the map
of Thebes.

DIONYSOS.
Pentheus, you've done me wrong, yet

I warn you yet again, do not take arms
Against a god.

PENTHEUS (*begins to plot the attack.*)

You escaped from prison, let that suffice you.
Or else I'll take you first, before your women.
DIONYSOS.
Stay quiet. Safe, Bromius will not let you
Drive his women from the hills.
PENTHEUS.
If you had ever borne responsibility for
Law and order anywhere you might be worth
Attention. Since you have not
Be less glib with your advice.
DIONYSOS.
And yet I offer only sane advice.
Sacrifice to this god. It is futile
To rage and kick against such power.
You are a man.
PENTHEUS.
All the sacrifice your god will have already
Lies in the glades of Kithairon. His women
Have been lavish. The state has nothing more to offer.
DIONYSOS.
And for this you raise the army of Thebes –
Against women?
PENTHEUS.
Those are not women. They are alien monsters
Who have invaded Thebes. I have a duty to preserve
The territorial integrity of Thebes.
DIONYSOS.
You will actually *attack* them Pentheus?
Draw sword, bow, cast spears, drive
Your armoured chariots into them?

PENTHEUS.

> They will have a chance to surrender
> Peacefully. If not – think who began the violence.
> Thebes must take measures for her own safety.

DIONYSOS.

> Thebes' well-being lies in acceptance
> Of this god. Your way leads to defeat,
> An ignominious rout. Bronze shields are no match
> For women's hands.

PENTHEUS.

> Will no man rid me of this pestilential tongue?
> All it does is wag. Whatever I do or say
> It's all the same. Yakkity – yak – yak – yak!

DIONYSOS.

> But there is a better way than yours. I ask
> Only for a chance to prove it.

PENTHEUS *ignores him, concentrates on plotting his campaign.*

> I will bring the women here,
> Without use of force.

PENTHEUS.

> Brilliant. This is the great
> Master plan, the grand deception.

DIONYSOS.

> You are too distrustful. I wish you well.
> I want you, and Thebes, to keep whole.

PENTHEUS *has finished. He looks satisfied, prepared. Turns to the* GUARDS.

PENTHEUS.

> Bring out my armour. And you – (*TO* DIONYSOS.)
> Be quiet. I am not a simpleton.

DIONYSOS (*stops the* GUARDS).

> Wait! (*He moves close to* PENTHEUS.) You could see them.
> I mean, there, up in the hills.

PENTHEUS.

Your mind is always busy, but I thought you
Cleverer. Any fool can see that trap.

DIONYSOS.

Why do you fear me Pentheus?

PENTHEUS.

Fear? I, son of Ichion?

DIONYSOS.

Yes, you are afraid of me.

PENTHEUS.

Because I will not follow you into a trap?

DIONYSOS.

No. It goes deeper. I saw it from our first encounter.

PENTHEUS.

If you refer to your cheap conjurer tricks
Don't let that swell your head. I have seen
Greater spectacles in market-places, greater feats
Of illusion. But now my mind is clear. I know you
For a charlatan. Perhaps a spy, an agent
Of subversion for some foreign power. Certainly
A degenerate, quite contemptible. Fear you?
Rid your mind of such conceit.

DIONYSOS.

But you do fear me. You fear my presence here
May set you free.

PENTHEUS.

Me? Who is the prisoner – you or I?

DIONYSOS.

You Pentheus, because you are a man of chains. You love
chains. Have you uttered one phrase today that was not
hyphenated by chains? You breath chains, talk chains, eat
chains, dream chains, think chains. Your world is bound in
manacles. Even in repose you are a cow chewing the cud, but
for you it is molten iron issuing from the furnace of your
so-called kingly will. It has replaced your umbilical cord and

issues from this point . . . *He touches him on the navel, commences to turn* PENTHEUS *round and round, gently. In spite of himself* PENTHEUS *is quite submissive.*) . . . and winds about you all the way back into the throat where it issues forth again in one unending cycle. (*He holds out his hand before* PENTHEUS' *eyes, like a mirror.*) Look well in the mirror Pentheus. What beast is it? Do you recognise it? Have you ever seen the like? In all your wanderings have your eyes ever been affronted by a creature so gross, so unnatural, so obscene?

With a superhuman effort PENTHEUS *shakes off his hypnotic state, tries to snatch the 'mirror' but clutches at nothing. He backs off, his face livid.*

PENTHEUS. Try that trick again! Touch our person once more and it won't be mere chains for you this time. How dare you!

DIONYSOS. Again chains. You are so scared I shall cut through that chain and set you at liberty.

PENTHEUS (*to the* GUARD). Has no one brought my armour? (*To* DIONYSOS.) Better keep your hacksaw for yourself. You shall need it before long.

DIONYSOS. Hacksaw. Your thoughts are so metallic. Dionysos loosens chains by gentler means.

PENTHEUS. I know what those are.

DIONYSOS. Tell me Pentheus, wouldn't you give a lot to know the future – not yours, you have none – but the future of this god Dionysos. It's a short cut, but . . . would you? Would you like to see something of his fate, the past and future legends of Dionysos – don't talk – look!

In the direction in which he points, a scene lights up. Wedding Scene. Music. The bridal procession enters, masked. The mask is the half-mask for the bridal retinue. The group register variations of hauteur, their clothes and attitude denote sixty-carat nobility, probably trade. The BRIDE *is veiled.*

An altar to Aphrodite is set at the entrance. The BRIDE'S FATHER *pauses by it, is handed a jug by a servant and pours libation at its base. He hands the jug to the* BRIDE *who also pours libation, makes a silent prayer. They proceed on to an elevated throne. A* SERVANT-GIRL *brings wine, is waved away by the aristocratic front-liners. She finds takers in the very rear.*

By the time she gets there the BRIDEGROOM *arrives. His retinue is one, a sort of* BESTMAN. *The* BRIDEGROOM *is clumsy, awkwardly dressed for the occasion in what must be his Sunday best.* BESTMAN *makes last-minute adjustments to* BRIDEGROOM's *attire, pulls him back in time to the altar, where the jug has been left. In his nervousness he takes a swig, then hastily pours a libation. In the hall he is waved unceremoniously to a seat almost at the feet of the bridal group. He sweats, his collar (or whatever) is too tight. This is a creature who is not comfortable in clothes.*

The masks from on high turn on him and inspect him coldly. We can almost hear the sigh of resignation as they turn away.

GUESTS *arrive, perfunctorily spilling a little libation. The wedding feast begins. Dancers perform. The* BRIDEGROOM *grows more and more uncomfortable. The* SERVANT-GIRL *carries on a quiet flirtation with him, doesn't wait for his cup to empty before refilling it. The* BRIDEGROOM *visibly responds to both charm and blandishments.*

A sudden clash of cymbals. All movements stop. Ceremonially the BRIDE'S FATHER *rises, unveils the* BRIDE. *From all the* GUESTS, *hands and faces are lifted in unmistakable gestures of rapture. Except the* BRIDEGROOM. *On his face and on the face of his* BESTMAN *are expressions of horror. The* BRIDE *(also masked) is a picture of horrendous, irredeemable ugliness.*

A movement (of light?) turns our attention to the bust of Aphrodite. The face is coming off. Underneath, the mocking face of DIONYSOS. *He beams on the scene.*

The SERVANT-GIRL *is almost never away from the* BRIDEGROOM.

The performing dancers resume their jigs. The BRIDEGROOM
drinks. The BRIDE *transfers to and fro between devastating glares at
the* SERVANT-GIRL *and loving smirks at her groom. The* BRIDE-
GROOM *drinks more and more.*

Suddenly he leaps up, brushing aside the restraining arm of his
BESTMAN. *He strides among the dancers, stops the musicians and
gives them instructions. He begins to dance. Already, a transforma-
tion has commenced. The music quickens. He stops, flings off his mask
and garments. Underneath, the Dionysian fawn-skin. The bridal
group registers predictable shock at the scantiness. He begins to dance.
He DANCES!*

*The dance ends with a leap on to the bridal table, upside down, his
back to the shocked 'high table'. The* BRIDE *screams, the* BRIDE'S
FATHER *rises in fury. His lips move and, over an amplified system, the
historic exchange:*

FATHER-IN-LAW. Hippoclides, you have danced your wife away·
BRIDEGROOM (*a melon-sized grin on his face*). οὐ φροντις
'Γπποκλείδη Hippoclides – does-not-care!

A snap black-out, except on the altar of Aphronysos.

DIONYSOS' VOICE. Look Pentheus!

*A new scene to another side. Again a wedding scene, but a huge
contrast. All the noise – music, revellers, snatches of drunken singing –
comes from off. What we see is the traditional* CHRIST-FIGURE,
*seated, but his halo is an ambiguous thorn-ivy-crown of Dionysos. At
his feet a* WOMAN *kneels, annointing them. Behind him, embroidering,
is a slightly more elderly* WOMAN. *Her mask is beautiful and radiates
an internal peace.*

A WOMAN *enters, irate, with a pitcher under her arm. She frowns on
this scene and points angrily to the kneeling* WOMAN. *Turns the
pitcher upside down to indicate the problem. Her angry gestures*

*include the feminine logic (pace Fem. Lib.) that the wine shortage is
related to the idle foot-annointer. The* CHRIST-FIGURE *makes
peace, indicates that the pitcher should be filled with the contents of a
pot in a corner. Water is poured into the pitcher. He raises his hand,
blesses it and takes a cup and invites her to fill it from the pitcher.
Tastes, nods, passes the cup to the irate* WOMAN. *Her expression
changes to rapture. She passes the cup to the kneeling* WOMAN,
*embraces the man. All taste, all are full of wonder, love and forgive-
ness. General embraces. She hurries out. Noise from off indicates the
success of this wine. The* CHRIST-FIGURE *looks up, smiles beatifically
in the direction of the sound.*

The scene fades slowly, as lights come up on DIONYSOS *and*
PENTHEUS. DIONYSOS *is holding out a cup (the same as last seen)
to* PENTHEUS.

PENTHEUS (*taking it*).
    Was that . . . he? Your god?
DIONYSOS.
    Does it matter? Drink.
PENTHEUS.
    Can I see some more?

Slowly dreamily, PENTHEUS *raises the cup to his lips.*

DIONYSOS.
    You are a king. You have to administer.
    Don't take shadows too seriously. Reality
    Is your only safety. Continue to reject illusion.
PENTHEUS.
    I do.
DIONYSOS.
    You found me out. I have the gift
    Of magic, conjuring. But reality
    Awaits you on the mountains.
    Are you still afraid?

PENTHEUS.

No. What do you suggest?

DIONYSOS.

Come with me to the mountains. See for yourself.
Watch the Maenads, unseen. There are risks
A king must take for his own people.

PENTHEUS.

Yes, yes, that is true.

DIONYSOS.

You are king. Your blood provides its own
Immunity. Just the same, if I may suggest it –
It is foolhardiness to take avoidable risks. . . .

PENTHEUS.

Go on. I am interested in your scheme. I find
Somehow, you are trustworthy. Your ways
Are strange, but . . . go on.

DIONYSOS.

You must not be recognised. Cunning proves
Always more successful than a show of force. You must
Wear a disguise.

PENTHEUS.

Yes, yes, I could dress as a common soldier,
Or a peasant, a herdsman . . . where is that cowherd?
I'll borrow his clothes.

DIONYSOS.

You forget. He and his sycophantic companions
Fomented this trouble. The sight of a herdsman now. . . .

PENTHEUS.

True, true. How shall I go then? I long
To see them at their revels.

DIONYSOS.

Do you? Then trust me. I shall lead you there
Safely.

PENTHEUS.

And stay to bring me back? I may get lost.

I know so little of Thebes beyond the city.
Almost nothing come to think of it.

DIONYSOS.

Your mother will bring you back, in triumph,
Leading a great procession. You will make your peace
With Dionysos.

PENTHEUS.

Oh, oh, not so fast. But I'll come with you.
I shall do as you say – short of surrender
To your priest of sly subversion.

DIONYSOS.

Then come disguised as one of those we go
To spy upon.

PENTHEUS.

What! Dress myself as a Maenad? A woman?
Make the throne a laughing-stock in Thebes?

DIONYSOS.

Suppose the madness had not left them?

PENTHEUS.

Don't mention it again. It is too undignified.

DIONYSOS.

Even more undignified it is to be severed
Limb from limb.

PENTHEUS.

Forget it, I will not bring myself
Down to such a mockery of the throne.
I shall go as I am, or not at all.

DIONYSOS.

As you wish. But wear your armour at least.
It may deflect a stone or two. Why seek bruises
From foolhardiness.

He turns to the OLD SLAVE, *speaking with emphasis.*

Bring the king his armour. Bring out
His only protection against the Bacchae.

PENTHEUS.

Yes, I shall go up to the mountains as a king.
Alone. Except for you as guide.

DIONYSOS.

In your royal armour.

PENTHEUS.

Yes, I shall go with you in the battledress
Of a worthy king of Thebes.

DIONYSOS.

It is by far the best plan. And if the Maenads
Spy you out, your royal presence will recall
Your mother and her sisters back to their
True heritage.

The OLD SLAVE *returns – with a female Bacchae costume.*

Here. I'll help you dress.

DIONYSOS *begins to dress him.* PENTHEUS *strikes the customary
stance for when he is being armed by a retainer. The contrast is
pathetic.*

PENTHEUS (*as the first piece is slipped on*).

Strange, it feels so soft today. Hardly
Like bronze and steel.

DIONYSOS.

It is the wine. It does create that effect.

PENTHEUS.

And lighter. It has hardly any weight.

DIONYSOS.

Wine lightens all burdens. You will discover
How lightly you walk, how your steps quicken
And turn to dance.

PENTHEUS.

I feel it already. Hurry. You must restrain me
As we go. I feel I shall hardly conduct myself
As becomes a soldier and a king.

DIONYSOS.

> Trust me. I shall be your guide. There is a force
> That blinds all men to diadems, swords and sceptres.
> You feel the beginnings of it.

PENTHEUS (*as* DIONYSOS *fastens a jewelled brooch*).

> You are a dark horse, full of hidden talents.
> To look at you, one would hardly think you knew those
> Intricacies of an armour's chains and buckles
> Yet you handle them like a practised armourer.
> Is there anything you don't know?

DIONYSOS.

> Dionysos taught me all I know.

PENTHEUS (*chuckles, in very good humour*).

> It is instructive to meet a fanatic. I could use
> Such loyalty. Whatever I say is turned
> And exploited by you to glorify Dionysos. (*He tilts the cup.*)
> Is there more of this nectar? I feel
> A great thirst within me

DIONYSOS (*stretching his hand*).

> Your cup is full.

PENTHEUS (*looks*).

> Ah. (*Takes a prolonged draught.*)

FIRST BACCHANTE.

> Look! He stands in the gate of the trap
> He'll find the Bacchae and with his life
> He'll answer. He thrashes in the net
> Of Dionysos, his wits are distracted
> Though he fought with the will of a Titan.
> Yet, for all that, he's a man.

DIONYSOS.

> Some hair still shows beneath your head-piece
> Not very soldierly – I'll tuck it in.

Places a wig on his head and ties it with a ribbon.

OLD SLAVE.

>He stands at the gate of retribution,
>The tyrant. Shall I pity him? I do not know.
>His thoughts are dislodged, his reason slithers.
>What sane mind struts in woman's clothing
>And thinks it an armour of bronze.

BACCHANTE.

>He'll raise a howl of derision all through Thebes
>Mincing like a camp-follower.

DIONYSOS.

>Dionysos will admit he's met his match
>To see such a figure of Ares walking the earth.

BACCHANTE.

>Once he mouthed fearsome threats. Now,
>He is dressed, a docile lamb, for a descent
>Into Hades. A rough caress by his mother
>Will ease him there.

SLAVE.

>A jealous joy, a ferocious, gentle joy
>Is my Dionysos.

BACCHANTE.

>Consummate god, most terrible, most gentle
>To mankind.

PENTHEUS.

>Mind you, I shall not forgive Tiresias,
>Or my grandfather. They should have set
>A good example and saved me all this bother.

DIONYSOS.

>You will meet them on your way. Your grandfather
>Shall be cruelly punished. And Agave. . . .

PENTHEUS.

>She most especially. My own mother –
>What a disgrace! I hope we don't find her
>Doing something really disgusting at those revels
>I would be forced to kill her – for the honour

Of the the house of Kadmos – you understand?

DIONYSOS.

Of course. Keep still while I fix this stubborn –
There, it's in ... About Agave, set your mind
At rest. I shall bring reconciliation to
Mother and Son. You shall return, Pentheus
Cradled in your mother's arms.

Slow commencement of light changes.

FIRST BACCHANTE.

Night – will it ever come
When what we know is done?
I seek release to a calm
Of green hills, white thighs
Flashing in the grass
The dew-soaked air kissing my throat.

SLAVE LEADER.

Night, night, set me free
Sky of a million roe, highway of eyes
Dust on mothwing, let me ride
On ovary silences, freely
Drawn on the reins of dreams.

BACCHANTE.

... the dance of night
Where darkness is deepest.

SLAVE LEADER.

Come, dawn, in the dance of the sun.
Come dawn, herald of the new order.

BACCHANTE.

But gently, as the dance of the young deer, swathed
In emerald meadow, when the terror of the hunt is past
The leap over knotted nets, the hunter's shrieks
Forgotten. Let the new order bring peace,
Repose, plenitude. ...

BACCHANTE.

... the lull

Of a sweet mothering copse, a timeless shade
Where no danger lurks. . . .

DIONYSOS (*still tucking in and tricking out* PENTHEUS, *his mouth is full of pins and clips*).

Is your wish still white-hot for a peep
At the forbidden? I would hate to take this trouble
Over nothing. Is your resolve still as strong as ever?

PENTHEUS (*with just a touch of tipsiness*).

Yes, but listen. I seem to see two suns
Blazing in the heavens. And now two Thebes
Two cities, each with seven gates. And you –
Are you a bull? There are horns newly
Sprouted from your head. Have you always been
A bull? Were you . . . (*He searches foggily in his brain.*)
                    . . . yes, that bull, in there?

Was it you?

DIONYSOS.

Now you see what you ought to see. Dionysos
Has been good to you with his gift of wine.

PENTHEUS.

Funny. Inside, I went this way with my head
Then, that way – back, forward – back. It was
Almost a kind of trance. I dreamed I stabbed
A bull. A minotaur. Was that you?

DIONYSOS.

I am whole. There – all that agitation has made
Your cuirass come loose. And the knee-guard.
Keep still till they are strapped in position.

He adjusts his sash, dolls out the pleats of his dress.

PENTHEUS.

I shall make you my armourer, after this campaign.

OLD SLAVE.

What does it mean, life? Dare one
Hope for better than merely warring, seeking

Change, seeking the better life? Can we
Control what threatens before the eruption?
Defeat what oppresses by anticipation? Can we?
Dare we surrender to what comes after, embrace
The ambiguous face of the future? It is enough
To concede awareness of the inexplicable, to wait
And watch the unfolding.

SLAVE.

For there are forces not ruled by us
And we obey them
Trust them. Though they travel inch by inch
They arrive.

OLD SLAVE.

Dionysos? Or – Nothing.
Not even a word for these forces.
They lack a name. We will call them
Spirits,
Gods

SLAVE.

Principles,
Elements,

ANOTHER.

Currents,
Laws, Eternal Causes.

ANOTHER.

But they are born in the blood
Unarguable, observed and preserved before time . . .

SLAVE LEADER.

As freedom. No teaching implants it
No divine revelation at the altar.
It is knotted in the blood, a covenant from birth.

DIONYSOS (hands PENTHEUS a thyrus).

Your sword. (PENTHEUS sticks it through the sash.)
Perfect. If your mind matches your appearance,
Then the enemies of Thebes have surprises to come.

PENTHEUS (*straighter than ever with a conscious militaristic preening*).

  I feel superhuman. I could hoist the whole of Kithairon
  On one shoulder – with valleys full of women
  Despite their dancing and madness . . . yes?

DIONYSOS.

  I do not doubt it. We'll find a hiding place
  That suits you best.

PENTHEUS.

  Take me right through Thebes
  Right through the centre. I am the only man here
  With dare and courage.

DIONYSOS.

  Yes, you alone
  Make sacrifices for your people, you alone.
  The role belongs to a king. Like those gods, who yearly
  Must be rent to spring anew, that also
  Is the fate of heroes.

PENTHEUS.

  We'll march through Thebes. I lately imported
  A famed drill-master for the troops. An expert.
  He hails, I think, from . . . Phrygia! Hey, that's you.
  Do you know him? Is he your countryman?

DIONYSOS.

  It is possible.

PENTHEUS.

  He's taught a new march to the household cavalry
  A masterpiece of precision. We'll prance through
  Thebes like those splendid horsemen. Wait,
  I'll teach you the movements. It's simple –
  Watch my feet!

He draws his 'sword', performs a brief salute forwards and sideways, then strikes a dance pose.

  Here we go –

One-Two-Back, One-Two-Back, One-Two-Back . . .

Exactly like TIRESIAS. *The music of Dionysos accompanies him welling in volume as* PENTHEUS *throws himself passionately into the dance, exhorting* DIONYSOS's *efforts.*

That's it. Very good. A little higher at the knees.
You're light on your feet I must say, quite
An accomplished dancer. Well, shall we advance?
DIONYSOS.
Forward Pentheus?
PENTHEUS (*lets off a loud yodel*).
Death to the Bacchae!
One-Two-Back! One-Two-Back! One-Two-Back!

His voice dies off in the distance, punctuated to the last by fierce yodels. DIONYSOS *stands and speaks with more than a suspicion of weariness from this now concluding conflict. It is not entirely a noble victory.*

DIONYSOS.
At last he comes, my Bacchantes
Prepare, you sisters, daughters of Kadmos
Agave, open your mothering arms –
Take him. Mother him. Smother him with joy.

Exit DIONYSOS. *As his speech ends, part of the* SLAVE CHORUS *sets up a dog-howl, a wail of death. Instantly a section separate themselves, move throughout the next speeches until they are joined up with the* BACCHANTES. *They form, for this last part, a solid fanatic front with the followers of Dionysos. The progress across should not be a dance, but a terse series of dramatic motions which takes its motif from the following invocation the decisive gesture of throwing their lot with the* BACCHANTES, *the casting off of the long vassalage in the House of Pentheus.*

SLAVE LEADER.
A self-swollen and calloused soul

Tumoured and hard,
All your malignant growths of thought
Level now, pare, and crop
They move in the dark with a fading glimmer
The ruler is overruled
You countered and strove at your peril
Seeking Dionysos. Death follows your finding.

BACCHANTE.

Go, track to the mountains
Swift hounds of madness
Run, dogs run,
Find the daughters of Kadmos

SLAVE (*separating*).

Snap at their dancing heels
Sink your fangs into their brains
Then turn them loose
Turn them loose on the foolhardy
Ruler, who spies in flapping skirts.

ANOTHER.

He's mad for the secret
He spies on the faithful possessed
His mother shall see him first
She'll cry to the Maenads.

BACCHANTE.

LOOK! See what creeps across the hill-side

Begins a stylised mime of the hunt. It ends just before the 'coup de grace' at the entry of the OFFICER. Only three or four of the BACCHANTES take part.

What creature is this?
What monstrous obscenity!
It surely was born of no woman
It took life from a rotting foetus
That heaved from a dying gorgon.

SLAVE.

Watch him sniffing up our mountains
Watch him drag like the spawn of a reptile.

ANOTHER.

Now we shall see the balance restored
O Justice! O Spirit of Equity, Restitution
Be manifest! A sharp clear sword
With blood on its edge – drive
To the gullet of Pentheus.

BACCHANTE.

Intent with sick passion
His mind is a sewer rat
Rooting and sniffing to the living heart
Madly assailing, profaning
The rites of the mother of god

A steady beat of the chant of 'Bromius Bromius' *by the* BACCHANTES *commences as counter-point to the dog-howl of the remnant* SLAVE CHORUS, *gradually gaining ascendancy until the arrival of the messenger.*

SLAVE LEADER.

Come, god
Of seven paths: oil, wine, blood, spring, rain
Sap and sperm, O dirge of shadows, dark-shod feet
Seven-ply crossroads, hands of camwood
Breath of indigo, O god of the seven roads
Farm, hill, forge, breath, field of battle
Death and the recreative flint . . .

SLAVE.

He runs, against the unassailable,
Runs, with violence against his, my
Forever-free spirit, unchainable,
He runs, with chains in his hand
With manacles for the encounter –
Death will counter his inventions

Death will end him!

OLD SLAVE (*remaining with the* SLAVE CHORUS).

Headlong he runs to his death
The gods do humble us with death
Lest we forget
We are not such as gods are made of
I say accept, accept.
Humility is wise, is blessed
There are great things unfathomable
The mind cannot grasp them.

SLAVE.

Where do we seek him? Where find him?
Where conflict rages, where sweat
Is torrents of rain, where flesh springs
Of blood fill him with longing as the rush
Of wine. There seek the hunter god.

SLAVE LEADER.

Justice! Restitution! O Spirit of Equity
Be manifest! Bright clear sword, a gleam
Of blood on its edge – drive!
Destroy the earth – spurning evil spawn of Ichion.

FIRST BACCHANTE.

Reveal yourself Dionysos! Be Manifest!
O Bacchus come! Come with your killing smile!
Come, a dragon with swarming heads, vomiting flames!
Come hunter, cast your noose.
Bring him down. Trample him
Underfoot with the herd of justice, your Maenads!
Bromius come! Master! Lover! Bull with horns
Of fire. Serpent with fangs of love. Lion
In my breasts, Eternal Ember in my hearth
Hunt this game to ground. Come Bromius!

Enter the OFFICER *from Kithairon just as the arm of the miming*
BACCHANTE *is raised to strike the 'quarry'.*

OFFICER

What is this? Has this god not done enough
That you still call here on Bromius?

Gradual silence. They turn to him.

In this house lived people who were once
The envy of all Greece – once – a family begun
In dragon's teeth, a summer harvest reaped
By Kadmos. It is winter now for this great race
I see no future spring.

VARIOUS.

What is it?
Have you news? Were you in the hills.

OFFICER.

I am only a soldier, nothing more, yet
I mourn the fortunes of this fallen house.
King Pentheus, son of Ichion, is dead.

BACCHANTE.

All power to Bromius! Victory on this first day
Of his homecoming. Quickly, how did he die?

OFFICER.

What is this? You dare rejoice
At the disasters of this house! My master
Is – DEAD!

SLAVE.

Your master not mine.
I have another home, another life.
Nor will the fear of dungeons stop me
Manifesting my joy.

OFFICER.

Your feelings can be forgiven. But this,
This exultation over terrible misfortune –
It's ugly.

BACCHANTE.

Was it truly terrible? Did you see?

OFFICER.

>There were three of us in all: Pentheus, and I
>Attending the king, and that stranger who offered
>His services as guide. Soon we left behind us
>The last outlying farms of Thebes, forded
>The Aesopus, then struck into the barren scrubland
>Of Kithairon.

>There, we halted in a grassy glen
>Unmoving, wordless, taking all precaution
>Not to be discovered. It was there we saw them
>In a sudden meadow carved in rockface of the cliffs
>Water ran freely there, and the pines grew dense
>With shade – there the Maenads rested, their hands
>Busy with their normal tasks, singing. They were
>Weird, disturbing tunes.

>But our king, Pentheus
>Unhappy man, found his view obscured by springy
>Undergrowth. 'Stranger,' he said, 'from here I can see
>Little of these counterfeiting worshippers.
>What if I climbed that towering fir that overhangs
>The banks, do you think I might see them better at
>Their shameless orgies?'

>And now the stranger worked a miracle!
>He reached up to the highest branch of a great fir
>Bent it down, down to the dark earth
>Till it was curved, a drawn bow in giant hands
>A wooden rim bent to encase a wheel for the chariot
>Of the sun. I was awed. No mortal could have done this.
>He seated Pentheus on the highest tip and,
>With great control he eased aloft the trunk
>Slowly, gently, most careful not to throw our king
>From his new throne among the leaves.
>And that fir rose, towering back to heaven
>With my master proudly seated at the top

You know that saying – a man the people seek
To roast, rubs himself in oil, crouches beside an open fire
Moaning, I have a chill: the rest is soon told.
The stranger had vanished. Only his voice, a bull's roar
Filled the mountains, stayed to set his doom in train.
'Maenads, look up!' it bellowed. They obeyed. The women
Saw King Pentheus stark against the sky
Clearer than he could see them. Hell broke loose.
Like startled doves, through grove and torrent
Over jagged rocks they flew, their feet excited
By the breath of god.

                His mother took the lead.
I heard the voice of Agave calling on her Maenads
To make a circle, shouting, 'This climbing beast
Must not escape lest he reveal the secrets
Of our god.' They made a ring. A hundred hands
A hundred supple arms heaved and strained. King Pentheus
Clutched at futile anchors on his naked nest
Hoping to keep death at bay. I heard the wrench of roots
From their long bed of earth and rocks. The fir was
Lifted out, it rose from earth, tilted, and down
From his high perch fell Pentheus, tumbling
Down to earth, sobbing and screaming as he fell.
He knew the end was near. His mother
First at the sacrifice of her own son
Fell upon him, angry priestess at the rites of death.
Pentheus, still miraculously alive, tore off wig,
And snood, touched her face and hoped for recognition.
He mouthed a last despairing plea in silence, his voice
Broken from the fall.

                She foamed at the mouth, her eyes
Rolled with frenzy. Agave was mad, stark mad
Possessed by Bacchus, blind to all plea for pity.
She seized the waving arm by the wrist, then

Planted her foot upon his chest and pulled,
Tore the arm clean off the shoulder. The tongue
Of Pentheus stretched out in agony, his mouth ran blood
But no sound came. Ino, on the other side of him
Began to peel his flesh. Then Autonoe, the swarming
Horde of Maenads homed on him, his other arm
Was torn, a foot flew up in the air, still encased
Within his sandals. The last I saw, his rib-case
Dragged, clawed clean of flesh. They played
With lumps of flesh, tossed from hand to blood-stained
Hand until the hills and valleys of Kithairon
Were strewn with fragments of his body.

The pitiful remains lie scattered
One piece among sharp rocks, others
Lost among the leaves in forest depths.
His mother soon seized the head, impaled it on a wand
And seems to think it is a mountain lion's head
She bears in triumph through the thickness of
Kithairon. She calls on Bromius: he is her 'fellow-huntsman'
'Comrade of the chase', she is 'crowned with victory'.
All the victory you will find on her is that grisly prize
And her own loss.

I must go. Best to flee
This place before the caryatid of grief returns and
Proves flesh and blood in the hour of truth.
Let who can console the house of Kadmos. (*Exit.*)

OLD SLAVE.
The ways of god are hard to understand
We know full well that some must die, chosen
To bear the burden of decay, lest we all die –
The farms, the wheatfields, cattle, even the
Vineyards up on the hills. And yet, this knowledge
Cannot blunt the edge of pain, the cruel
Nature of this death. Oh this is a heartless

Deity, bitter, unnatural in his revenge.
To make a mother rip her son like bread
Across a banqueting board! I pity her.

SLAVE LEADER.

Who pities us? When the mine-prop falls and pulps
Our bones with mud, who pities us? When harvest
Fails, who goes without? And you, if you had
Died at the feast of Eleusis, would Thebes
Have remembered you with pity?

OLD SLAVE.

I pity her. But I fear she'll prove
Beyond mortal consolation

FIRST BACCHANTE.

Look! Here she comes, the priestess
Of hunting rites. Take her, enfold the new triumphant
Bride of Bromius.

AGAVE *runs in with her trophy stuck on a thyrsus but invisible under gold ribbons. She raises the stave and the ribbons flow around her as she runs once round the stage.*

AGAVE.

Women of the hills . . . Bacchae!

CHORUS.

Speak Agave! Welcome!

AGAVE.

Do you see this bough, this fresh-cut
Spray from the mountains? Observe
How it streams. Can you see it?

CHORUS.

We see it Agave.

FIRST BACCHANTE.

We know it Agave and for this
We sing your praise. Tell us of the hunt.
We've heard of the snarling beast whose towering
Pride was humbled by the might of Bromius

AGAVE.

>Have you known a mountain lion
>Wild-fanged, red-eyed indomitable whelp
>Have you known such savagery ever
>Trapped without net or noose? Without
>Weapons, without beaters or other
>Time-consuming subterfuge. Answer me.

CHORUS.

>It's unheard-of.

AGAVE.

>Then look on this? Look at the prize.
>Is it noble?

OLD SLAVE.

>It is royal Agave. Where did you find it?

AGAVE.

>On the mountains of Kithairon. Happy,
>Happy was the hunting!

OLD SLAVE.

>Who killed him?

AGAVE.

>I, Agave. I struck first, tore off
>A limb that launched its unsheathed claws
>Against my face. Thus – my foot was planted
>Crushing its rib-case! I heard sweet sounds of sinews
>Yielding at the socket as I tugged. The beast's snarl
>Turned to agony. I swung its lifeless limb
>Up in the air, the first taste of the hunt
>To Dionysos. The Maenads call me
>Agave the Blest.

BACCHANTE.

>Blessed Agave, thrice blessed daughter of Kadmos!

OLD SLAVE.

>Tell the rest Agave.

AGAVE.

>All the daughters of Kadmos are blest.

Ino, Autonoe came after. But mine was the first
Hand on the quarry. *I* struck the death-blow.
Later, we rested. My sisters wove a worthy
Garland for the noble prize. See how it flows,
A god-like mane for a royal beast. It flows evenly, richly
Like my golden joy.

OLD SLAVE.

Joy indeed. Joyful Kadmos, Joyful Thebes.

AGAVE.

All must share in my glory. I summon you all
To a feast of celebration.

OLD SLAVE.

A feast . . .? Oh Agave.

SLAVE LEADER.

To eat of this – lion, Agave?

AGAVE.

This bull, lion, this swift mountain-goat
This flash of the wind in grassland,
This dew-skinned deer. . . .

Oh, our god is generous
Cunningly, cleverly, Bacchus the hunter
Launched the Maenads on his prey.

OLD SLAVE.

Yes, he is a great hunter. He knows

The way to a death-hunt of the self.

AGAVE.

Ah, you praise him now.

CHORUS.

We praise Dionysos.

AGAVE.

And the blessed Agave?

CHORUS.

We praise the blessed Mother.

OLD SLAVE.

And your son?

AGAVE.

Will praise the Mother who caught
And offered the sacrifice.
  Oh he'll wear his pride
As palpably as mine, his joy will mount
In full flood-tide higher than – mine.
I feel a strength in me like the purity
Of Dionysos. And here is the proof –
This boon of our chase, this golden gift
Of Dionysos.

OLD SLAVE.

Then poor woman, unshroud this great prize
Show the citizens of Thebes this trophy
Of the god of joy.

AGAVE.

Why? Can't they see it? (*She looks up at the thyrsus.*)
    Ah! The shroud of gold
Obscures him. Maenads! Catch this billowing mane.

She takes the thyrsus in both hands and whirls it. The MAENADS
chase and catch the ribbons as they unfurl and float outwards. With
AGAVE *in the centre, a Maypole dance evolves naturally from their*
positions. It is a soft graceful dance.

Men and women of Thebes, the city of high
Towers, impregnable, behold the trophy of your –
Women, captured in the hunt. Behold our offering
To this year of Dionysos. We tracked him down
Not with nets nor spears forged in workshops
Of Thessaly, but with untried, delicate hands
That give birth. What are they worth, those clumsy
Tools you fabricate, your armour and swords?
We caught this beast, we brought him to the altar,
Our fair mothers' hands our only weapons. Tell me

Do you know of any greater than the power
Of our creative wombs?

But . . . where is father?
He should be here. And my son, Pentheus?
Fetch them someone. And bring a ladder too.
I want it set against the wall. This masthead must
Fly high upon our palace walls.

Exit the SLAVE LEADER. *A* BACCHANTE *relieves* AGAVE *at the Maypole and she takes her place. The* SLAVE LEADER *re-enters with a ladder, stands watching for some moments. Then shouts above the noise. He sets the ladder in position and shouts above the music.*

SLAVE LEADER (*a mock-bow*).
The ladder, Queen Mother, Agave!

She looks up, rushes back and snatches the thyrsus and 'flies' up the ladder with it.

Enter KADMOS *supported by* TIRESIAS *followed by attendants who carry a covered bier, the remnants of* PENTHEUS.

KADMOS.
This way . . . follow me. Is the burden heavy?
My grief is heavier. Set him down, there
Before the palace.
Pentheus has come home.
It was a long, weary search, there was so much
Of my dismembered son, and set so wide apart
Through the forest. No two pieces in a single place.
Tiresias and I, we had paid our tribute to Dionysos
And were back in the city. The news found us here
Of this unseasonable harvest reaped upon the mountains.
Oh the mountains of Kithairon boast a gory crop!
Unlucky house . . . I saw them at the mountainside
Aristaus' wife, mother of Actaeon, Autonoe and Ino
All still stung with madness. Agave I hear
Is still possessed . . . what was in their minds?

What moved them to do this thing? Why couldn't . . .
    (*Violently.*)
She should have known him! (*Raising his head, he sees her.*)
                                    No . . . no . . .
I don't want to see!

TIRESIAS.
    What is it Kadmos?

AGAVE (*turning from her task*).
    Did I hear . . .? Ah, you at last. No! Don't look.
    Turn around. Wait until this silken mane is
    Fully displayed in all its splendour. Then you can tell me
    How it looks from there? No royal wall
    Ever boasted ornament to equal this.
    Have rumours reached you yet? If not
    I have such news for you. You are the proud
    Father of brave daughters. I tell you, nowhere
    Can such prowess be excelled. We have left our
    Shuttle in the loom, raised our sights
    To higher things. We hunt. We kill. Now, look!
    A royal masthead! Look Father. Turn around!
    Glory in my kill, my new-found prowess, invite
    All Thebes to a great celebration. You are blessed father
    By this great deed of mine.

KADMOS.
    Oh gods, can I measure grief like this?
    I cannot look. This is awful murder, child.
    This, this is the noble victim you have slaughtered
    To the gods? To share this *glory* you invite
    All Thebes and me.
                        Oh Gods!
    How terribly I pity you and then myself.
    The things you've done, the horror, the abomination,
    Oh fling your thanksgiving before what deity you please
    Not ask my grief to come and celebrate!
    Celebrate. . . . (*He breaks down.*)

Dionysos is just. But he is not fair!
Though he had right on his side, he lacks
Compassion, the deeper justice. And he was born
Here. This . . . is his home . . . this soil gave him breath.

AGAVE *comes down slowly, right up to him.*

AGAVE.

    Oh look at him old, sourpuss. Monopoly
    Of the sacrificial knife passes
    Into women's hands
    And turns him crabbed and sour.
    I hope Pentheus takes after me, and wins as I
    The laurels of the hunt when he goes hunting
    With the younger men of Thebes. Alas, all he does
    Is quarrel with god. You should talk to him.
    You're the one to do it. Yes, someone call him out
    Let him witness his mother's triumph.

KADMOS (*anguished*).

    You'll know. You must! You'll see the horror
    In your deed, then pain will wring blood from your eyes
    Though, if I could grant . . . a boon . . . I would
    You never woke up from your present state until
    You die. It won't be happiness, but . . .
    You'll feel no pain.

AGAVE.

    Why do you reproach me? Is something wrong?

KADMOS.

    Look up at the sky

AGAVE *obeys.*

AGAVE.

    So? What do you expect me to see?

KADMOS.

    Does it look the same to you? Or has it changed?

AGAVE.

    It seems . . . somehow . . . clearer, brighter than before.

There is a red glow of sunset, the colour of blood.

KADMOS.

And inside you, do you still
Feel the same sense of floating?

AGAVE.

Floating? No. And it's quieter . . . restful.
I feel . . . a sense of changing. The world
No longer heaves as if within my womb.
There was a wind too but . . . I think it's . . . dropped.

KADMOS.

Can you still hear me? Do you know what I'm saying?
Do you remember what you said before?

AGAVE.

I . . . no. What were we talking about?

KADMOS.

Who was your husband?

AGAVE.

Ichion, born they say of the dragon seed.

KADMOS.

And the name of the child you bore him?

AGAVE.

Pentheus?

KADMOS.

Is he living?

AGAVE.

Assuredly.

KADMOS.

Now look up at the face you've set
Upon that wall. Whose head is it?

AGAVE.

Whose . . .? (*Violently.*) It's a lion!
It's . . . I . . . think . . .

KADMOS.

Look at it. Look directly at it.

AGAVE.

No. What is it? First tell me what it is.

KADMOS.

You must look. Look closely and carefully.

She brings herself to obey him.

AGAVE.

Oh. Another slave? But why did I nail it
Right over the entrance?

KADMOS.

Closer. Move closer. Go right up to it.

She moves closer until she is standing almost directly under it, looking up. She stiffens suddenly, her body shudders and she whirls round screaming.

AGAVE.

Bring him down! Bring him down! Bring him . . .

KADMOS *has moved closer, and she collapses onto his shoulders sobbing.*

KADMOS (*to the* SLAVES).

Bring down the head.

But they all retreat and look down, as if they dare not touch him. After a while KADMOS realises that no one has moved to obey him.

Did no one hear me? Take down my son!

AGAVE (*suddenly calmer*).

Let no hand but mine be laid on him.
I am his mother. I brought him out to life
I shall prepare him for his death.

She turns towards the ladder, stops.

How did he die?

KADMOS.

He mocked the god Dionysos, spied on his Mysteries.

He goes towards the bier and lifts a corner of the cover.

Here is his body. A long weary search
I gathered him together, piece by piece
On the mountains of Kithairon.

AGAVE.

Kithairon . . . but . . .

KADMOS.

Where Actaeon was torn to pieces.

AGAVE.

And Pentheus?

KADMOS.

The whole city was possessed by Dionysos.
He drove you mad. You rushed to the mountains . . .

AGAVE.

Of Kithairon? Yes . . . was I not there?

KADMOS.

You killed him.

AGAVE.

I?

KADMOS.

You and your sisters. You were possessed.

AGAVE (*a soft sigh*).

A-ah.

She stands stock-still, then turns towards the ladder.

It is time to bring him down. (*Begins to climb, slowly.*)

KADMOS.

Console her Tiresias. I no longer understand
The ways of god. I may blaspheme.

TIRESIAS.

Understanding of these things is far beyond us.
Perhaps . . . perhaps our life-sustaining earth
Demands . . . a little more . . . sometimes, a more
Than token offering for her own needful renewal.
And who, more than we should know it? For all too many
The soil of Thebes has proved a most unfeeling

Host, harsh, unyielding, as if the dragon's teeth
That gave it birth still farms its subsoil.
They feel this, same as I, even through calloused soles.
O Kadmos, it was a cause beyond madness, this
Scattering of his flesh to the seven winds, the rain
Of blood that streamed out endlessly to soak
Our land. Remember when I said, Kadmos, we seem to be
Upon sheer rockface, yet moisture oozes up at every
Step. Blood you replied, blood. His blood
Is everywhere. The leaves of Kithairon have turned red
    with it.

KADMOS (*the cry is wrung from him*).
    Why us?

AGAVE (*her hands are on* PENTHEUS' *head, about to lift it. Quietly*).
    Why not?

The theme music of Dionysos wells up and fills the stage with the god's presence as a powerful red glow shines suddenly as if from within the head of PENTHEUS, *rendering it near-luminous. The stage is bathed in it instantly, from every orifice of the impaled head spring red jets, spurting in every direction. Reactions of horror and panic.* AGAVE *screams and flattens herself below the head, hugging the ladder.*

TIRESIAS.
    What is it Kadmos? What is it?

KADMOS.
    Again blood Tiresias, nothing but blood.

TIRESIAS (*feels his way nearer the fount. A spray hits him and he holds out a hand, catches some of the fluid and sniffs. Tastes it*).
    No. It's wine.

Slowly, dreamlike, they all move towards the fountain, cup their hands and drink. AGAVE *raises herself at last to observe them, then tilts her head backwards to let a jet flush full in her face and flush her mouth. The light contracts to a final glow around the heads of* PENTHEUS *and* AGAVE.

A slow curtain.